THE
GOLDEN FLEECE

A Romance

JULIAN HAWTHORNE

The Golden Fleece

Julian Hawthorne

© 1st World Library, 2007
PO Box 2211
Fairfield, IA 52556
www.1stworldlibrary.com
First Edition

LCCN: 2007934150

Softcover ISBN: 978-1-4218-9654-0
Hardcover ISBN: 978-1-4218-9754-7
eBook ISBN: 978-1-4218-9554-3

Purchase *"The Golden Fleece"*
as a traditional bound book at:
www.1stWorldLibrary.com/purchase.asp?ISBN=978-1-4218-9654-0

1st World Library is a literary, educational organization
dedicated to:

- Creating a free internet library of downloadable ebooks

- Hosting writing competitions and offering book publishing
  scholarships.

Interested in more 1st World Library books? contact:
literacy@1stworldlibrary.com
Check us out at: www.1stworldlibrary.com

1st World Library Literary Society

Giving Back to the World

"If you want to work on the core problem, it's early school literacy."

- James Barksdale, former CEO of Netscape

"No skill is more crucial to the future of a child, or to a democratic and prosperous society, than literacy."

- Los Angeles Times

"Literacy... means far more than learning how to read and write... The aim is to transmit... knowledge and promote social participation."

- UNESCO

"Literacy is not a luxury, it is a right and a responsibility. If our world is to meet the challenges of the twenty-first century we must harness the energy and creativity of all our citizens."

- President Bill Clinton

"Parents should be encouraged to read to their children, and teachers should be equipped with all available techniques for teaching literacy, so the varying needs and capacities of individual kids can be taken into account."

- Hugh Mackay

CHAPTER I

The professor crossed one long, lean leg over the other, and punched down the ashes in his pipe-bowl with the square tip of his middle finger. The thermometer on the shady veranda marked eighty-seven degrees of heat, and nature wooed the soul to languor and revery; but nothing could abate the energy of this bony sage.

"They talk about their Atlantises,—their submerged continents!" he exclaimed, with a sniff through his wide, hairy nostrils. "Why, Trednoke, do you realize that we are living literally at the bottom of a Mesozoic—at any rate, Cenozoic —sea?"

The gentleman thus indignantly addressed contemplated his questioner with the serenity of one conscious of freedom from geologic responsibility. He was a man of about the professor's age,—say, sixty years,—but not like him in appearance. His figure was stately and massive,—that of one who in his youth must have possessed vast physical strength, rigidly developed and disciplined. Well set upon his broad shoulders was a noble head, crowned with gray, wavy hair; the eyes and eyebrows were black and powerful, but the expression was kindly and humorous. His moustache and the Roman convexity of his chin would have confirmed your conviction that he was a retired warrior; in which you would have been correct, for General Trednoke always appeared what he was, both outwardly and inwardly. His great frame, clad in white linen, was comfortably disposed in a Japanese straw arm-chair; yet there was a soldierly poise in his attitude. He was smoking a large and excellent cigar; and a cup of coffee, with a tiny glass of cognac beside it, stood on a mahogany stand at his elbow.

"Do you remember, Meschines, the time I licked you at school?" he inquired, in a tone of pleasant reminiscence.

"I can't say I do. What's more, I venture to challenge your statement. And though you are a hundred pounds the better of me in weight, and a West Point graduate, I will wager my pipe (which is worth its weight in diamonds) against that old woollen shirt of Montezuma's that you showed me yesterday, that I can lick you to-day, and forget all about it before bedtime!"

"Well, I guess you could," returned the general, with a little chuckle, "even if I hadn't that Mexican bullet in my leg. But you couldn't, forty-five years ago, though you tried, and though I was a year younger than you, and weighed five pounds less. Come, now: you don't mean to say you've forgotten Susan Brown!"

"Oh—ah—hah! Susan Brown! Well, I declare! And what brought her into your head, I should like to know?"

"Why, after breaking your heart first, and then mine, I lost sight of her, and I don't think I have seen her since. But it appears she was married to a fellow named Parsloe."

"Don't fancy that name!" observed the professor, wagging his head and frowning. "Has a mean sound to it. But what of it?"

"Well, she died,—rest her soul!—and Parsloe too. But they had a daughter, and she survives them."

"And resembles her mother, eh?—No, Trednoke, the time for that sort of thing has gone by with me. Susan might have had me, five-and-forty years ago; but I can't undertake to revive my passion for the benefit of Mrs. Parsloe's daughter. Besides, I'm too busy to think of marriage, and not—not old enough!"

At this tour de force, the general laughed softly, and finished his coffee. An old Indian, somewhat remarkable in appearance, with shaggy white hair hanging down on his shoulders, stepped forward from the room where he had been waiting, and removed the cup.

"No letters yet, Kamaiakan?" asked the general, in Spanish.

"In a few minutes, general," the other replied. "Pablo has just come in sight over the hill. There were several errands."

"Muy buen!—I was going to say, Meschines, her father and mother left the girl poor, and she, being, apparently, clever and energetic, took to—"

"I know!" the professor interrupted. "They all do it, when they are clever and energetic, and that's the end of them!—School-teaching!"

"Not at all," returned General Trednoke. "She entered a dry-goods store."

"Entered a dry-goods store! Well, there's nothing so extraordinary in that. I've seen quantities of women do it, of all ages, colors, and degrees. What did she buy there?"

"Oh, a fiddlestick!" exclaimed the general. "Why don't you keep quiet and listen to my story? I say, she went into a great dry-goods store in New York, as sales- woman."

"Bless my soul! You don't mean a shop-girl?"

"That's what I said, isn't it? And why not?"

"Oh, well!—but, shade of Susan Brown! Ichabod!—what is the feminine of Ichabod, by the way, Trednoke? But, seriously, it's too bad. Susan may have been fickle, but she was always aristocratic. And now her daughter is a shop-girl. You and I are avenged!"

"You are just as ridiculous, Meschines, as you were thirty or fifty years ago," said the general, tranquilly. "You declaim for the sake of hearing your own voice. Besides, what you say is un-American. Grace Parsloe, as I was saying, got a place as shop-girl in one of the great New York stores. I don't say she mightn't have done worse: what I say is, I doubt whether she could have done better. That house—I know one of its founders, and I know what I'm talking about—is like an enormous family, where children are born, year after year, grow up, and take their places in life according to their quality and merit. What I mean is, that the boy who drives a wagon for them to-day, at three dollars a week, may control one of their chief departments, or even become a partner, before they're done with him; and, mutatis mutandis, the same with the girls. When these girls marry, it's apt to be into a higher rank of life than they were born in; and that fact, I take it, is a good indication that their shop-girl experience has been an education and an improvement. They are given work to do, suited to their capacity, be it small or great; they are in the way of learning something of the great economic laws; they learn self- restraint, courtesy, and—"

"And human nature! Yes, poor things: they see the American buying-woman, and that is a discipline more trying than any you West Pointers know about! Oh, yes, I see your point. If the fathers of the big family ARE fathers, and the children ARE children to them . . . All the same, I fancy the young ladies, when they marry into the higher social circles, as you say they do, don't, as a rule, make their shop girl days a topic of conversation at five-o'clock teas, or put 'Ex-shop-girl to So-and-so' at the bottom of their visiting-cards."

"I believe, after all, you're a snob, Meschines," said the general, pensively. "But, as I was about to say, when you interrupted me ten minutes ago, Grace Parsloe is coming on here to make us a visit. She fell ill, and her employers, after doing what could be done for her in the way of medical attendance, made up their minds to give her a change of climate. Now, you know, as she had originally gone to them with a letter from me, and as I live out here, on the borders of the Southern desert, in a climate that has no equal, they naturally thought of writing to me about it. And of course I said I'd be delighted to have her here, for a month, or a year, or whatever time it may be. She will be a pleasure to me, and a friend for Miriam, and she may find a husband somewhere up or down the coast, who will give her a fortune, and think all the better of her because she, like him, had the ability and the pluck to make her own way in the world."

"Humph! When do you expect her?"

"She may turn up any day. She is coming round by way of the Isthmus. From what I hear, she is really a very fine, clever girl. She held a responsible position in the shop, and—"

"Well, let us sink the shop, and get back to the rational and instructive conversation that we—or, to be more accurate, that I was engaged in when this digression began. I presume you are aware that all the indications are lacustrine?"

Hereupon, a hammock, suspended near the talkers, and filled with what appeared to be a bundle of lace and silken shawls, became agitated, and developed at one end a slender arched foot in an open-work silk stocking and sandal-slipper, and at the other end a dark, youthful, oval face, with glorious eyes and dull black hair. A voice of music asked,—

"What is lacustrine, papa?"

"Oh, so you are awake again, Senorita Miriam?"

"I haven't been asleep. What is lacustrine?"

"Ask the professor."

"Lacus, you know, my dear," said the latter, "means fresh-water indications as against salt."

"Then how does Great Salt Lake—"

"Oh, for that matter, the whole ocean was fresh originally. Moisture, evaporation, precipitation. Water is a great solvent: earthquakes break the crust, and there you are!"

"Then, before the earthquakes, the Salt Lakes were fresh?" rejoined the hammock.

"There was fresh water west of the Rockies and south of— Why," cried the professor, interrupting himself, "when I was in Wyoming and around there, this spring, in what they call the Bad Lands,—cliffs and buttes of indurated yellow clay and sandstone, worn and carved out by floods long before the Aztecs started to move out of Canada,—I saw fossil bones sticking out of the cliffs, the least of which would make the fortune of a museum. That was between the Rockies and the Wahsatch."

"People's bones?" asked the hammock, agitating itself again, and showing a glimpse of a smooth throat and a slender ankle.

"Bless my soul! If there were people in those days they must have had an anxious time of it!" returned the sage. "No, no, my dear. There was brontosaurus, and atlantosaurus, and hydrosaurus, and iguanodon,—lizards, you know, not like these little black fellows that run about in the pulverized feldspar here, but chaps eighty or a hundred feet long, and twenty or thirty high; and turtles, as big as a house."

"How did they get there?"

"Got mired while they were feeding, perhaps; or the water drained off and left them high and dry."

"But where did the water go to?"

The general chuckled at this juncture, and lit another cigar. "She knows more questions than you do the answers to them," quoth he. "But I wouldn't mind hearing where the water went to, myself. I should like to see some of it back again."

"Ask the earthquakes, and the sun. There's a hundred and thirty degrees of heat in some of these valleys,—abysses, rather, three or four hundred feet below sea- level. The earth is very thin-skinned in this region, too, and whatever water wasn't evaporated from above would be likely to come to grief underneath."

"But, professor," said the musical voice, "I thought there was a law that water always seeks its own level. So how can there be empty places below sea-level?"

"It's the fault of the aneroid barometer, my dear. We were very comfortable and commonplace until that came along and revealed anomalies. The secret lies, I suppose, in the trend of the strata, which is generally north and south. You see the ridges cropping out all through the desert; and there's a good deal of lava oozing over them, too. They probably act as walls, to prevent the sea getting in from the west, or the Colorado leaking in from the east."

"In that case," remarked the general, "a little more seismic disturbance might produce a change."

"It would have to be more than a little, I suspect," returned Meschines.

"Kamaiakan told me that the Indians have a prophecy that a great lake will come back and make the desert fruitful, and that there are some who know the very place where the water will begin to flow." And here the hammock, with a final convulsion, gave birth to a beautiful young woman, in a diaphanous silk dress and a white lace mantilla. She crossed the veranda, and seated herself on the broad arm of her father's chair.

"Why, that's important!" said the general, arching his brows. "I wonder if Kamaiakan is one of those who know the place? If so, it might be worth his while to let me into the secret."

"Oh, you couldn't go there! It's enchanted, and people who go near it die. There are bones all about there, now."

"This Kamaiakan appears to be a remarkable personage:

Julian Hawthorne

where did you pick him up?" inquired the professor.

"It was rather the other way," Trednoke replied, taking one of his daughtcr's hands in his, and caressing it. "We are appendages to Kamaiakan. You look so natural, sitting there, Meschines, that I forget it's thirty years since we met, and that all the significant events of my life have happened in that time,—the Mexican war, my marriage, and the rest of it! I have been a widower ten years."

"And I've been a bachelor for over sixty!" said Meschines, with a queer expression. "Your wife was Spanish, was she not?"

"Her father was a Mexican of Andalusian descent. But her mother was descended from the race of Azatlan: there are records and relics indicating that her ancestors were princes in Tenochtitlan before Cortez made trouble there."

"And I've been losing my heart to a princess, and never realized my audacity!" exclaimed the professor, laying his hand on his waistcoat and making an obeisance to Miriam.

She tossed her free foot, and played with the fringe of her reboso.

"I will tell my maid to look for it," she said; "but I think you must have left it in papa's curiosity-room."

"No: I'm an Aztec sacrifice!" cried the professor; and they all laughed. "One would hardly have anticipated," he resumed after a pause, addressing Trednoke, "that you would have made a double conquest,—first of the men, and then of the woman!"

"The woman conquered me, without trying or wishing to,

and then, because she was a woman, took compassion on me. Whether my country has benefited much by the Mexican annexation, I can't say; but I know Inez—made a heaven on earth for me," concluded the general, in a low voice. His countenance, at this moment, wore a solemn and humble expression, beautiful to see; and Miriam bent and laid her cheek against his. Meschines knocked the ashes out of his pipe, and sighed.

"No woman ever took compassion on me," he remarked, "and you see the result, —ashes!"

"Ashes,—with their wonted fires living in them," said Trednoke.

"We were talking about this Indian of yours," said Meschines.

"Ay, to be sure. Well, he was attached to Inez's family when I first knew them. It was a peculiar relation; not like that of a servant. One finds such things in Mexico. The conquered race were of as good strain as their conquerors; the blood of Montezuma was as blue as the best of the Castilian. There were many intermarriages; and there are many instances of the survival of traditions and records; though the records are often symbolic, and would have no meaning to persons not initiated. But they have been sufficient to perpetuate ties of a personal nature through generation after generation; and the alliance between Kamaiakan and Inez was of this kind. His forefathers, I imagine, were priests, and priests were a mighty power in Tenochtitlan. For aught I know, indeed Kamaiakan may be an original priest of Montezuma's; no one knows his age, but he does not look an hour older, to-day, than when I first saw him, over twenty years ago."

"He must be!" said Miriam, with some positiveness. "He has

Julian Hawthorne

told me of seeing and doing things hundreds of years ago. And he says—" She paused.

"What does he say, Nina adorada?" asked her father.

"It was about the treasure, you know."

"Let us hear. The professor is one of us."

"It's one of our traditions that my mother's ancestors, at the time of Cortez, were very rich people," continued Miriam, glancing at Meschines, and then letting her eyes wander across the garden, blooming with roses and fragrant with orange-trees, and so across the trellised vines towards the soft outline of the mountains eastward. "A great part of their wealth was in the form of jewels and precious stones. When Cortez took the city, one of the priests, who was a relative of our family, put the jewels in a box, and hid them in a certain place in the desert."

"And does Kamaiakan know where the place is?" asked the general.

"He can know, when the time comes."

"Which will be, perhaps, when you are ready for your dowry," observed the professor, genially.

"A spell was put upon the spot," Miriam went on, with a certain imaginative seriousness; for she loved romance and mystery so well, and was of a temperament so poetical, that the wildest fairy-tales had a sort of reality for her. "No one can find the treasure while the spell remains. But Kamaiakan understands the spell, and the conjuration which dissolves it; and when he dissolves it, the treasure will be found."

"And, between ourselves," added the general, "Kamaiakan is himself the priestly relative by whom the spell was wrought. He bears an enchanted life, which cannot cease until he has restored the jewels to Miriam's hands."

"There might be something in it, you know," said Meschines, after a pause. "The treasures of Montezuma have never been found. Is there no old chart or writing, in your collection of curiosities and relics, that might throw light on it?"

"The scriptures of Anahuac were of the hieroglyphic type,— picture-writing," replied the other. "No, I fear there is nothing to the purpose; and if there were, I shouldn't know how to decipher it."

"But, papa, the tunic!" exclaimed Miriam.

"Oh! has the tunic anything to do with it?"

"Is that the queer woollen garment with the gold embroidery?" inquired the professor, becoming more interested. "I took a fancy to that, you remember. Has it a story?"

"Well, it is a kind of an anomaly, I believe," the general answered, looking up at his daughter with a smile. "The Aztecs, you are aware, dressed chiefly in cotton. Even their defensive armor was of cotton, thickly quilted. Their ornaments were feathers, and embroidery of gold and precious stones. But wool, for some reason, they didn't wear; and yet this garment, as you can see for yourself, is pure wool; and that it is also pure Aztecan is beyond question."

"Admitting that, what clue does it give to the treasure?"

"You must ask Kamaiakan," said Miriam: "only, he wouldn't tell you."

"Possibly," the professor suggested, "the place where the treasure is hidden is the place whence the water is to flow out; and the water is the treasure."

"Seriously, do you suppose that such a phenomenon as the return of an inland sea is physically practicable?" asked Trednoke.

"No phenomenon, in this part of the world, would surprise me," returned Meschines. "The Colorado might break its barriers; or it is conceivable that some huge stream, taking its rise in the heights hundreds of miles north and east of us, may be flowing through subterranean passages into the sea, emerging from the sea-bottom hundreds of miles to the westward. Now, if a rattling good earthquake were to happen along, you might awake in the morning to find yourself on an island, or even under water."

"A moderate Mediterranean would satisfy me," the general said. "I wouldn't exchange the certainty of it for the treasures of Montezuma."

"The thirst for gold and for water are synonymous in your case?"

"Give this section a moist climate, and I needn't tell you that the Great American Desert would literally blossom as the rose. Even as it is, I expect a great deal of it will be redeemed by scientific irrigation. The soil only needs water to become inexhaustibly productive. Our desert, as you know, is not sand, like parts of the Sahara; it has all the ingredients that go to nourish plants, only their present powdery condition makes them unavailable. Now, I can, to-day, buy a hundred square miles of desert for a few dollars. You see the point, don't you?"

"And all you want is expert opinion as to the likelihood of finding water?"

"The man who solves that question for me in the affirmative is welcome to half my share of the results that would ensue from it."

"Why don't you engage some expert to investigate?"

"One can't always trust an expert. I don't mean as to his expertness only, but as to his good faith. He might prefer to sell the idea to somebody who could pay cash, —which I cannot."

"Why, you seem to have given this thing a good deal of thought, Trednoke."

"Well, yes: it has been my hobby for a year past; and I have made some investigations myself. But this is the first time I have spoken of it to any one."

"I understand. And what of the investigations?"

"I can say that I found enough to interest me. I'll tell you about it some time. I should be glad to leave Miriam something to make her independent."

"I should say that her Creator had already done that!" said Meschines. "By the way, I know a young fellow—if he were only here—who is just the man you want, and can be trusted. He's a civil engineer,—Harvey Freeman: the Lord only knows in what part of the world he is at this speaking. He has made a special study of these subterranean matters."

"Don't you remember, papa, Coleridge's poem of Kubla Khan?—

　　　　Julian Hawthorne

"Where Alph, the sacred river, ran
Through caverns measureless to man
Down to a sunless sea!"

"Our sacred river, when we find it, shall be named Miriam."

"It ought to be Kamaiakan," she rejoined; "for, if anybody finds it, it will be he."

"I think I hear the wings of the angel of whom we have been speaking," said the general. "Yes, here he is; and he has got the letters. Let us see! One for you Meschines. And this, I see, is from our friend Miss Parsloe, postmarked Santa Barbara. Why, she'll be here to-morrow, at that rate."

"Here's a queer coincidence!" exclaimed the professor, who had meanwhile opened his envelope and glanced through the contents. "The very man I was speaking of,—Harvey Freeman! Says he is in this neighborhood, has heard I'm here, and is coming down to pay me a visit. Methinks I hear the rolling of the sacred river!"

"But you won't mention it to him, until—"

"Bless me! Of course not. I'll bring him over here, in the course of human events, and you can take a look at him, and act on your own intuitions. I won't say on Princess Miriam's, for Harvey is a very fine- looking fellow, and her intuitions might get confused."

"A civil engineer!" said Miriam, with an intonation worthy of the daughter of a West-Pointer and the descendant of an Aztec prince.

Kamaiakan (who spoke only Spanish) had been gathering up some cushions that had fallen out of the hammock. Having replaced them, and cast a quick glance at Meschines, he withdrew.

Julian Hawthorne

CHAPTER II

The Southern Pacific Railway passes, today, not far from the site of General Trednoke's ranch. But the events now to be narrated occurred some years before the era of transcontinental railroads: they were in the air, but not yet bolted down to the earth. The general, therefore, was a pioneer, and was by no means overrun with friends from the East in search of an agreeable winter climate. The easiest way to reach him—if you were not pressed for time—was round the cape which forms the southernmost point of South America and sticks its sharp snout inquiringly into the Antarctic solitudes, as if it scented something questionable there. The speediest route, though open to strange discomforts, was by way of the Isthmus; and then there were always the saddle, the wagon, and the stage, with the accompaniments of road-agents, tornadoes, deserts, and starvation.

Miss Grace Parsloe came via the Isthmus; and the latter part of her journey had been alleviated by the society of a young gentleman from New York, Freeman by name. There were other passengers on the vessel; but these two discovered sympathies of origin and education which made companionship natural. They sat together at table, leaned side by side over the taffrail, discussed their fellow-travellers, and investigated each other. As he lolled on the bench with folded arms and straw hat tilted back from his forehead she, glancing side-long, as her manner was, saw a sunburnt aquiline nose, a moustache of a lighter brown than the visage which it decorated, a lean, strong jaw, and a muscular neck. His forehead, square and impending, was as white as ivory in comparison with the face below; his hair, in accordance with the fashion introduced by the late war, was cropped close. But what especially moved Miss Grace were those long, lazy blue eyes, which seemed to tolerate everything, but to be interested in nothing,—hardly even in her. Now, Grace could not help knowing she was a pretty girl, and it was somewhat of a novelty to her that Freeman should appear so indifferent. It would have been difficult to devise a better opportunity than this to monopolize masculine admiration, and she fell to speculating as to what sort of an experience Mr. Freeman must have had, so to panoply him against her magic. On the other hand, she was the recipient of whatever attentions he could bring himself to detach from the horizon-line, or from his own thoughts (which appeared to amount, practically, to about the same thing). She had no other rivals; and a woman will submit amiably to a good deal of indifference, provided she be assured that no other woman is enjoying what she lacks.

Freeman, for his part, had nothing to complain of. Grace Parsloe was a singularly pretty girl. Singular properly qualifies her. She was not like the others,—by which phrase he epitomized the numerous comely young women whom he had, at various times and in several countries, attended, teased, and kissed. Both physically and mentally, she was very fine-wrought. Her bones were small; her body and limbs were slender, but beautifully fashioned. She was supple and vigorous. Grace is a product of brain as well as an effect of bodily symmetry: Grace had the quality on both counts. She answered to one's conception of Mahomet's houris, assuming that the conception is not of a fat person. Her head was small, but well proportioned,—compact as to the forehead, rather broad across the cheek-bones, thence tapering to the chin. Her eyes were blue, but of an Eastern strangeness of shape and setting; they were subject to great and sudden changes of expression, depending, apparently, on the varying state of her emotions, and betraying an intensity more akin to the Oriental temperament than to ours. There was in her something subtle and fierce; yet overlaying it, like a smooth and silken skin, were the conventional polish and bearing of an American school graduate. She was, in deed, noticeably artificial and self-conscious in manner and in the intonations of her speech; though it was an aesthetic delight to see her move or pose, and the quality of her voice was music's self. But Freeman, after due meditation, came to the conclusion that this was the outcome of her recognition of her own singularity: in trying to be like other people, she fell into caricature. Freeman, somehow, liked her the better for it. Like most men of brain and pith, who have seen and thought much, he was thankful for a new thing, because, so far as it went, it renewed him. It pleased him to imagine that he could, with a word or a look, cause this veil of artifice to be thrown aside, and the primitive passion and fierceness behind it to start forth. He allowed himself to imagine, with a certain satisfaction, that were he to make this young woman jealous she would think nothing of thrusting a dagger between his ribs. Reality,—what a delight it is! The actual touch and feeling of the spontaneous natural creature have been so buried beneath centuries of hypocrisy and humbug that we have ceased to believe in them save as a metaphysical abstraction. But even as water, long depressed under-ground in perverse channels, surges up to the surface, and above it, at last, in a fountain of relief, so Nature, after enduring ages of outrage and banishment, leaps back to her rightful domain in some individual whom we call extraordinary because he or she is natural. Grace Parsloe did not seem (regarded as to her temperament and quality) to belong where she was: therefore she was a delightful incident there. Had she been met with in the days of the Old Testament, or in the depths of Persia or India at the present time, even, she might have appeared commonplace. But here she was in conventional costume, with conventional manners. And, just as the nautch-girls, and other Oriental dancers and posturers, wear a costume which suggests nature more effectively than does nature itself, so did Grace's conventionality suggest to Freeman the essential absence of conventionality more forcibly than if he had seen her clad in a turban and translucent caftan, dancing off John the Baptist's head, or driving a nail into that of Sisera. Grace certainly owed much of her importance to her situation, which rendered her foreign and piquante. But, then, everything, in this world, is relative.

Racial types seem to be a failure: when they become very marked, the race deteriorates or vanishes. In the counties of England, after only a thousand years, the women you meet in the rural districts and country towns all look like sisters. The Asiatics, of course, are much more sunk in type than the Anglo-Saxons; and they show us the way we would be going. Only, there is hope in rapid transit and the cosmopolitan spirit, and especially in these United States, which bring together the ends of the earth, and place side by side a descendant of the Puritans like Freeman, and a daughter of Irak-Ajemi.

"What are you coming to California for, Mr. Freeman?"

Freeman had already told her what he had been in the Isthmus for,—to paddle in miasmatic swamps with a view to the possibility of a canal in the remote, speculative future. He had given her a graphic and entertaining picture of the hideous and inconceivable life he had led there for six months, from which he had emerged the only member of a party of nineteen (whites, blacks, and yellows) who was not either dead by disease, by violence, or by misadventure, or had barely escaped with life and a shattered constitution. Freeman, after emerging from the miasmatic hell and lake of Gehenna, had taken a succession of baths, with soap and friction, had been attended by a barber and a tailor, and had himself attended the best table to be found for love or money in the charming town of Panama. He had also spent more than half of the week of his sojourn there in sleep; and he was now in the best possible condition, physical and mental, —though not, he admitted, pecuniary. As to morals, they had not reached that discussion yet. But, in all that he did say, Freeman exhibited perfect unreserve and frankness, answering without hesitation or embarrassment any question she chose to ask (and she asked some curious ones).

But when she asked him such an innocent thing as what he was after in California—an inquiry, by the way, put more in idleness than out of curiosity—Freeman stroked his yellow moustache with the thumb of the hand that held his Cuban cigarette, gazed with narrowed eyelids at the horizon, and for some time made no reply at all. Finally he said that California was a place he had never visited, and that it would be a pity to have been so near it and yet not have improved the opportunity of taking a look at it.

Grace instantly scented a mystery, and was not less promptly resolved to fathom it. And what must be the nature of a mystery attaching to a handsome man, unmarried, and evidently no stranger to the gentler sex? Of course there must be a woman in it! Her eyes glowed with azure fire.

"You have some acquaintances in California, I suppose?" she said, with an air of laborious indifference.

"Well,—yes; I believe I have," Freeman admitted.

"Have they lived there long?"

"No; not over a few months. I accidentally heard from a person in Panama. I dropped a line to say I might turn up."

"She—you haven't had time to get an answer, then?"

Freeman inhaled a deep breath through his cigarette, tilted his head back, and allowed the smoke to escape slowly through his nostrils. In this manner, familiar to his deep-designing sex, he concealed a smile. Grace was, in some respects, as transparent as she was subtle. So long as the matter in hand did not touch her emotions, she had no difficulty in maintaining a deceptive surface; but emotion she could not disguise, though she was probably not aware of the fact; for emotion has a tendency to shut one's own eyes and open what they can no longer see in one's self to the gaze of outsiders.

"No," he said, when he had recovered his composure. "But that won't make any difference. We are on rather intimate terms, you see."

"Oh! Is it long since you have met?"

"Pretty long; at least it seems so to me."

Grace turned, and looked full at her companion. He did not meet her glance, but kept his profile steadily opposed, and went on smoking with a dreamy air, as if lost in memories and anticipations, sad, yet sweet.

"Really, Mr. Freeman, I hardly thought —you have always seemed to care so little about anything—I didn't suspect you of so much sentiment."

"I am like other men," he returned, with a sigh. "My affections are not given indiscriminately; but when they are given,—you understand,—I—"

"Oh, I understand: pray don't think it necessary to explain. I'm sure I'm very far from wishing to listen to confidences about another,—to—"

"Yes, but I like to talk about it," interposed Freeman, earnestly. "I haven't had a chance to open my heart, you know, for at least six months. And though you and I haven't known each other long, I believe you to be capable of appreciating what a man feels when he is on his way to meet some one who—"

"Thank you! You are most considerate! But I shall be additionally obliged if you would tell me in what respect I can have so far forgotten myself as to lead you to think me likely to appreciate anything of the kind. I assure you, Mr. Freeman, I have never cared for any one; and nothing I have seen since I left home makes it probable that I shall begin now."

"I am sorry to hear that," said Freeman, slowly drawing another cigarette out of his bundle, and beginning to re-roll it with a dejected air.

"Indeed!"

"Yes: the fact is, I had hoped that you had begun to have a little friendly feeling for me. I am more than ready to reciprocate."

"I hope you will spare me any insults, sir. I have no one to protect me, but—"

"I assure you, I mean no insult. You cannot help knowing that I think you as beautiful and fascinating a woman as I have ever met; but of course you can't help being beautiful and fascinating. Do I insult you by having eyes? If so, I am sorry, but you will have to make the best of it."

With this, he turned in his seat, and calmly confronted her. Beautiful she certainly was, at that moment; but it was the beauty of an angry serpent. She had a pencil in her hand, with which, a little while before, she had been sketching heads of some of the passengers in her little notebook. She was now handling this inoffensive object in such a way as to justify the fancy that, had it been charged with a deadly poison in its point, instead of with a bit of plumbago of the HH quality, she would have driven it into Freeman's heart then and there.

"Is it no insult," said she, in a sibilant voice, "to talk to me as you are doing, when you have just told me that you love another woman, and are going to meet her?"

Freeman's brows gradually knitted themselves in a frown of apparent perplexity. "I must say I don't understand you," he observed, at length. "I am quite sure I have said nothing of the sort. How could I?"

"If you wish to quibble about words, perhaps not. But was not that your meaning?"

"No, it wasn't. You are the only woman who has been in my thoughts to-day."

"Mr. Freeman!"

"Well?"

"You have intimated very clearly that you are engaged—married, for aught I know —to a woman whom you are now on your way to meet—"

At this point she stopped. Freeman had interrupted her with a shout of laughter.

She had been very pale. She now flushed all over her face, and jumped to her feet.

"Sit down," he said, laying a hand on her dress and (aided by a lurch of the vessel) pulling her into her seat again, "and listen to me. And then I shall insist upon an apology. This is too much!"

"I shall ask the captain—"

"You will not, I promise you. Look here! When I was in Panama, I met there a fellow I used to know in New York. He told me that he had recently crossed the continent with Professor Meschines, who used to teach geology and botany at Yale College, when he and I were students there. The professor had come over partly for the fun of the thing, and partly to look for specimens in the line of his profession. My friend parted from him at San Francisco: the professor was going farther south."

"What has all this to do with the woman who—"

"It has this to do with it,—that the professor is the woman! He is over sixty years old, and has always been a good friend of mine; but I am not going to marry him. I am not engaged to him, he is not beautiful, nor even fascinating, except in the way of an elderly man of science. And he is the only human being, besides yourself, that I know or have ever heard of on the Pacific coast. Now for your apology!"

Grace emitted a long breath, and sank back in her seat, with her hands clasped in her lap. She raised her hands and covered her face with them. She removed them, sat erect, and bent an open-eyed, intent gaze upon her companion.

After this pantomime, she exclaimed, in the lowest and most musical of tones, "Oh! how hateful you are!" Then she cried out with animation, "I believe you did it on purpose!" Finally, she sank back again, with a soft laugh and sparkling eyes, at the same time stretching out her right arm towards him and placing her hand on his, with a whispered, "There, then!"

Freeman, accepting the hand for the apology, kissed it, and continued to hold it afterwards.

"Am I not a little goose?" she murmured.

"You certainly are," replied Freeman.

"You mustn't hold my hand any more."

"Do you mean to withdraw your apology?"

"N—no; but it doesn't follow that—"

"Oh, yes, it does. Besides, when a man receives such a delicate, refined, graceful, exquisite apology as this,"—here he lifted the hand, looked at it critically, and bestowed another kiss upon it,—"he would be a fool not to make the most of it."

"Ah, I'm afraid you're dangerous. You are well named—Freeman!"

"My name is Harvey: won't you call me by it?"

"Oh, I can't!"

"Try! Would it make it easier if I were to call you by yours?"

"Mine is Miss Parsloe."

"Pooh! How can that be your name which you are going to change so soon? When I look at you, I see your name; when I think of you, I say it to myself,—Grace!"

"How do you know I am going to change my name soon—or ever?"

"Whom are you talking to?"

"To you,—Harvey! Oh!" She snatched her hand away and pressed it over her lips.

"How do I know you are beautiful, Grace, and—irresistible?"

"But I'm not! You're making fun of me! Besides, I'm twenty."

"How many times have you been engaged?"

"Never. Nobody wants to be engaged to a poor girl. Oh me!"

"Do you know what you are made of, Grace? Fire and flowers! Few men in the world are men enough to be a match for you. But what have you been doing with yourself all this time? Why do you come to a place like this?"

"Maybe I had a presentiment that . . . What nonsense we are talking! But what you said reminds me. It's the strangest coincidence!"

"What is it?"

"Your Professor Meschines—"

"On the contrary, he is a most matter- of-fact old gentleman."

"Do be quiet, and listen to me! When my mamma was a girl in school, there were two boys there,—it was a boy-and-girls' school,—and they were great friends. But they both fell in love with my mamma—"

"I can understand that," put in Freeman.

"How do you know I am like my mamma? Well, as I was saying, they both fell in love with her, and quarrelled with each other, and had a fight. The boy that won the fight is the man to whose house I am going."

"Then he didn't marry your mamma?"

"Oh, no; that was only a childish affair, and she married another man."

"The one who got thrashed?"

"Of course not. But the one who got thrashed is your Professor Meschines."

"I see! The poor old professor! And he has remained a bachelor all his life."

"Mamma has often told me the story, and that the Trednoke boy went to West Point, and distinguished himself in the Mexican war, and married a Mexican woman, and the Meschines boy became a professor in Yale College. And now I am going to see one of them, and you to see the other.

Isn't that a coincidence?"

"The first of a long series, I trust. Is this West-Pointer a permanent settler here?"

"Yes, for ever so long,—twenty years. He's a widower, but he has a daughter—Oh, I know you'll fall in love with her!"

"Is she like you?"

"I don't know. I've never seen her, or General Trednoke either."

"Come to think of it, though, nobody is like you, Grace. Now, will you be so good as to apologize again?"

"Don't you think you're rather exacting, Harvey?"

However, the apology was finally repeated, and continued, more or less, during the rest of the voyage; and Grace quite forgot that she had never made Harvey tell what was really the cause of his coming to California. But she, on her side, had a secret. She never allowed him to suspect that the past eighteen months of her life had been passed as employee in a New York dry- goods store.

CHAPTER III

General Trednoke's house was built by Spanish missionaries in the sixteenth century; and in its main features it was little altered in three hundred years. In a climate where there is no frost, walls of adobe last as long as granite. The house consisted, practically, of but one story; for although there were rooms under the roof, they were used only for storage; no one slept in them. The plan of the building was not unlike that of a train of railway-cars,—or, it might be more appropriate to say, of emigrant-wagons. There was a series of rooms, ranged in a line, access to them being had from a narrow corridor, which opened on the rear veranda. Several of the rooms also communicated directly with each other, and, through low windows, gave on the veranda in front; for the house was merely a comparatively narrow array of apartments between two broad verandas, where most of the living, including much of the sleeping, was done.

Logically, there can be nothing uglier than a Spanish-American dwelling of this type. But, as a matter of fact, they appear seductively beautiful. The thick white walls acquire a certain softness of tone; the surface scales off here and there, and cracks and crevices appear. In a damp country, like England, they would soon become covered with moss; but moss is not to be had in this region, though one were to offer for it the price of the silk velvet, triple ply, which so much resembles it. Nevertheless, there are compensations. The soil is inexhaustibly fertile, and its fertility expresses itself in the most inveterate beauty. Such colors and varieties of flowers exist nowhere else, and they continue all the year round. Climbing vines storm the walls, and toss their green ladders all over it, for beauty to walk up and down. Huge jars, standing on the verandas, emit volcanoes of lovely blossoms; and vases swung from the roof drip and overflow with others, as if water had turned to flowers. In the garden, which extends over several acres at the front of the house, and, as it were, makes it an island in a gorgeous sea of petals, there are roses, almonds, oranges, vines, pomegranates, and a hundred rivals whose names are unknown to the present historian, marching joyfully and triumphantly through the seasons, as the symphony moves through changes along its central theme.

Everything that is not an animal or a mineral seems to be a flower. There are too many flowers,—or, rather, there is not enough of anything else. The faculty of appreciation wearies, and at last ceases to take note. It is like conversing with a person whose every word is an epigram. The senses have their limitations, and imagination and expectation are half of beauty and delight, and the better half; otherwise we should have no souls. A single violet, discovered by chance in the by-ways of an April forest in New England, gives a pleasure as poignant as, and more spiritual than, the miles upon miles of Californian splendors.

Monotony is the ruling characteristic,—monotony of beauty, monotony of desolation, monotony even of variety. The glorious blue overhead is monotonous: as for the thermo-meter, it paces up and down within the narrowest limits, like a prisoner in his cell, or a meadow-lark hopping to and fro in a seven-inch cage. The plan and aspect of the buildings are monotonous, and so is the way of life of those who inhabit them. Fortunately, the sun does rise and set in Southern California: otherwise life there would be at an absolute stand-still, with no past and no future. But, as it is, one can look forward to morning, and remember the evening.

Then, there are the not infrequent but seldom very destructive earthquakes; the occasional cloud-bursts and tornadoes, sudden and violent as a gunpowder-explosion; and, finally, the astounding contrast between the fertile regions and the desert. There are places where you can stand with one foot planted in everlasting sterility and the other in immortal verdure. In the midst of an arid and hopeless waste, you come suddenly upon the brink of a narrow ravine, sharply defined as if cut out with an axe, and packed to the brim with enchanting and voluptuous fertility. Or you will come upon mountains which sweep upward out of burning death into sumptuous life. When the monotony of life meets the monotony of death, Southern California becomes a land of contrasts; and the contrasts themselves become monotonous.

General Trednoke's ranch was very near the borders of these two mighty forces. An hour's easy ride would carry him to a region as barren and apparently as irreclaimable as that through which Childe Roland journeyed in quest of the Dark Tower; lying, too, in a temperature so fiery that it coagulated the blood in the veins, and stopped the beating of the heart. Underfoot were fine dust, and whitened bones; the air was prismatic and magical, ever conjuring up phantom pictures, whose characteristic was that they were at the farthest remove from any possible reality. The azure sky descended and became a lake; the pulsations of the atmosphere translated themselves into the rhythmic lapse of waves; spikes of sage-brush and blades of cactus became sylvan glades, and hamlets cheerful with inhabitants. Only, all was silent; and as you drew near, the scene trembled, altered, and was gone!

Julian Hawthorne

Hideous black lizards and horned toads crawl and hop amid this desolation; and the deadly little sidewinder rattlesnake lies basking in the blaze of sunshine, which it distils into venom. Sometimes the level plain is broken up into savage ridges and awful canons, along whose arid bottoms no water streams. As you stagger through their chaotic bottoms, you see vast boulders poised overhead, tottering to a fall; a shiver of earthquake, a breath of hurricane, and they come crashing and splintering in destruction down. Along the sides of these acclivities extend long, level lines and furrows, marks of where the ocean flowed ages ago. But sometimes the hills are but accumulations of desert dust, which shift slowly from place to place under the action of the wind, melting away here to be re-erected yonder; mounding themselves, perhaps, above a living and struggling human being, to move forward, anon, leaving where he was a little heap of withered bones. A fearful place is this broad abyss, where once murmured the waters of a prehistoric sea. Let us return to the cool and fragrant security of the general's ranch.

At right angles to the main body of the house extend two wings, thus forming three sides of a square, the interior of which is the court-yard. Here the business of the establish-ment is conducted. It is the liveliest spot on the premises; though it is liveliness of a very indolent sort. The veranda built around these sides is twenty feet in breadth, paved with tiles that have been worn into hollows by innumerable lazy footsteps, mostly shoeless, for this side of the house is frequented chiefly by the servants of the place, who are Mexican Indians. Ancient wooden settles are bolted to the walls; from hooks hang Indian baskets of bright colors; in one corner are stretched raw hides, which serve as beds. Small brown children, half naked, trot, clamber, and crawl about. Black-haired, swarthy women squat on the tiled floor, pursuing their vocations, or, often, doing nothing at all beyond continuing a placid organic existence. Boys and men saunter in and out of the court-yard, chatting or calling in their musical patois; once in a while there is a thud and clatter of hoofs, a rider arriving or departing. It is an entertaining scene, charming in its monotony of small changes and evolutions; you can sit watching it in a half-doze for twenty years at a stretch, and it may seem only as many minutes, or vice versa.

Most of the rooms in the wings are used for the kitchens and other servants' quarters; but one large chamber is devoted to a special purpose of the general's own: it is a museum; the Curiosity-Room, he calls it. It is lighted by two windows opening on opposite sides, one on the court-yard, the other on an orange grove at the south end of the house. Besides being, in itself, a cool and pleasant spot, it is full of interest to any one who cares about the relics and antiquities of an ancient and vanishing race, concerning whom little is or ever will be known. There are two students in it at this moment; though whether they are studying antiquities is another matter. Let us give ear to their discourse and be instructed.

"But this was made for you to wear, Miss Trednoke. Try it. It fits you perfectly, you see. There can be no doubt about your being a princess, now!"

"I sometimes feel it,—here!" she said, putting her hand on her bosom. She was looking at him as she said it, but her eyes, instead of any longer meeting his, seemed to turn their regard inward, and to traverse strange regions, not of this world. "I see some one who is myself, though I can never have been she: she is surrounded with brightness, and people not like ours; she thinks of things that I have never known. It is the memory of a dream, I suppose," she added, in another tone.

"Heredity is a queer thing. You may be Aztecan over again,

in mind and temperament; and every one knows how impressions are transmitted. If features and traits of character, why not particular thoughts and feelings?"

"I think it is better not to try to explain these things," said she, with the unconscious haughtiness which maidens acquire who have not seen the world and are adored by their family. "They are great mysteries,—or else nothing." She now removed from her head the curious cap or helmet, ornamented with gold and with the green feathers of the humming-bird, which her companion had crowned her with, and hung it on its nail in the cabinet. "Perhaps the thoughts came with the cap," she remarked, smiling slightly. "I don't feel that way any more. I ought not to have spoken of it."

"I hope the time will come when you will feel that you may trust me."

"You seem easy to know, Mr. Freeman," she replied, looking at him contemplatively as she spoke, "and yet you are not. There is one of you that thinks, and another that speaks. And you are not the same to my father, or to Professor Meschines, that you are to me."

"What is the use of human beings except to take one out of one's self?"

"But it is not your real self that comes out," said Miriam, after a little pause. She never spoke hurriedly, or until after the coming speech had passed into her face.

Freeman laughed. "Well," he said, "if I'm a hypocrite, I'm one of those who are made and not born. As a boy, I was frank enough. But a good part of my life has been spent with people who couldn't be trusted; and perhaps the habit of protecting myself against them has grown upon me. If I

could only live here for a while it would be different.—
Here's an odd-looking thing. What do you call that?"

"We call it the Golden Fleece."

"The Golden Fleece! I can imagine a Medea; but where is the
Dragon?"

"If Jason came, the Dragon might appear."

"I remember reading somewhere that the Dragon was less to
be feared than Medea's eyes. But this fleece seems to have
lost most of its gold. There is only a little gold embroidery."

"It shows where the gold is hidden."

"It's you that are concealing something now, Miss Trednoke.
How can a woollen garment be a talisman?"

"The secret might be woven into it, perhaps," replied
Miriam, passing her fingers caressingly over the soft tunic.
"Then, when the right person puts it on, it would—But you
don't believe in these things."

"I don't know: you don't give me a chance. But who is the
right person? The thing seems rather small. I'm sure I
couldn't get it on."

"It can fit only the one it was made for," said Miriam,
gravely. "And if you wanted to find the gold, you would trust
to your science, rather than to this."

"Well, gold-hunting is not in my line, at present. Every
nugget has been paid for more than once, before it is found.
Besides, there is something better than gold in Southern
California,—something worth any labor to get."

"What is it?" asked Miriam, turning her tranquil regard upon him.

Harvey Freeman had never been deficient in audacity. But, standing in the dark radiance of this maiden's eyes, his self-assurance dwindled, and he could not bring himself to say to her what he would have said to any other pretty woman he had ever met. For he felt that great pride and passion were concealed beneath that tranquil surface: it was a nature that might give everything to love, and would never pardon any frivolous parody thereof. Freeman had been acquainted with Miriam scarcely two days, but he had already begun to perceive the main indications of a character which a lifetime might not be long enough wholly to explore. Marriage had never been among the enterprises he had, in the course of his career, proposed to himself: he did not propose it now: yet he dared not risk the utterance of a word that would lead Miriam to look at him with an offended or contemptuous glance. It was not that she was, from the merely physical point of view, transcendently beautiful. His first impression of her, indeed, had been that she was merely an unusually good example of a type by no means rare in that region. But ere long he became sensible of a spiritual quality in her which lifted her to a level far above that which can be attained by mere harmony of features and proportions. Beneath the outward aspect lay a profound depth of being, glimpses of which were occasionally discernible through her eyes, in the tones of her voice, in her smile, in unconscious movements of her hands and limbs. Demonstrative she could never be; but she could, at will, feel with tropical intensity, and act with the swiftness and energy of a fanatic.

In Miriam's company, Freeman forgot every one save her,— even himself,—though she certainly made no effort to attract him or (beyond the commonplaces of courtesy) to interest him. Consequently he had become entirely oblivious of the existence of such a person as Grace Parsloe, when, much to his irritation, he heard the voice of that young lady, mingled with others, approaching along the veranda. At the same moment he experienced acute regret at the whim of fortune which had made himself and that sprightly young lady fellow- passengers from Panama, and at the idle impulse which had prompted him to flirt with her.

But the past was beyond remedy: it was his concern to deal with the present. In a few seconds, Grace entered the curiosity- room, followed by Professor Meschines, and by a dashing young Mexican senor, whom Freeman had met the previous evening, and who was called Don Miguel de Mendoza. The senor, to judge from his manner, had already fallen violently in love with Grace, and was almost dislocating his organs of speech in the effort to pay her romantic compliments in English. Freeman observed this with unalloyed satisfaction. But the look which Grace bent upon him and Miriam, on entering, and the ominous change which passed over her mobile countenance, went far to counteract this agreeable impression.

One story is good until another is told. Freeman had really thought Grace a fascinating girl, until he saw Miriam. There was no harm in that: the trouble was, he had allowed Grace to perceive his admiration. He had already remarked that she was a creature of violent extremes, tempered, but not improved, by a thin polish of subtlety. She was now about to give an illustration of the passion of jealousy. But it was not her jealousy that Freeman minded: it was the prospect of Miriam's scorn when she should surmise that he had given Grace cause to be jealous. Miriam was not the sort of character to enter into a competition with any other woman about a lover. He would lose her before he had a chance to try to win her.

Julian Hawthorne

But fortune proved rather more favorable than Freeman expected, or, perhaps, than he deserved. Grace's attack was too impetuous. She stopped just inside the threshold, and said, in an imperious tone, "Come here, Mr. Freeman: I wish to speak to you."

"Thank you," he replied, resolving at once to widen the breach to the utmost extent possible, "I am otherwise engaged."

"Upon my word," observed the professor, with a chuckle, "you're no diplomatist, Harvey! What are you two about here? Investigating antiquities?"

"The remains of ancient Mexico are more interesting than some of her recent products," returned Freeman, who wished to quarrel with somebody, and had promptly decided that Senor Don Miguel de Mendoza was the most available person. He bowed to the latter as he spoke.

"You—a—spoken to me?" said the senor, stepping forward with a polite grimace. "I no to quite comprehend—"

"Pray don't exert yourself to converse with me out of your own language, senor," interrupted Freeman, in Spanish. "I was just remarking that the Spaniards seem to have degenerated greatly since they colonized Mexico."

"Senor!" exclaimed Don Miguel, stiffening and staring.

"Of course," added Freeman, smiling benevolently upon him, "I judge only from such specimens of the modern Mexican as I happen to meet with."

Don Miguel's sallow countenance turned greenish white. But, before he could make a reply, Meschines, who scented mischief in the air, and divined that the gentler sex must somehow be at the bottom of it, struck in.

"You may consider yourself lucky, Harvey, in making the acquaintance of a gentleman like Senor de Mendoza, who exemplifies the undimmed virtues of Cortez and Torquemada. For my part, I brought him here in the hope that he might be able to throw some light on the mystery of this embroidered garment, which I see you've been examining. What do you say, Don Miguel? Have these designs any significance beyond mere ornament? Anything in the nature of hieroglyphics?"

The senor was obliged to examine, and to enter into a discussion, though, of course, his ignorance of the subject in dispute was as the depths of that abyss which has no bottom. Miriam, who was not fond of Don Miguel, but who felt constrained to exceptional courtesy in view of Freeman's unwarrantable attack upon him, stood beside him and the Professor; and Freeman and Grace were thus left to fight it out with each other.

But Grace had drawn her own conclusions from what had passed. Freeman had insulted Don Miguel. Wherefore? Obviously, it could only be because he thought that she was flirting with him. In other words, Freeman was jealous; and to be jealous is to love. Now, Grace was so constituted that, though she did not like to play second fiddle herself, yet she had no objection to monopolizing all the members of the male species who might happen, at a given moment, to be in sight.

She had, consequently, already forgiven Freeman for his apparent unfaithfulness to her, by reason of his manifest jealousy of Don Miguel. As a matter of fact, he was not jealous, and he was unfaithful; but fate had decreed that there should be, for the moment, a game of cross-purposes; and the decrees of fate are incorrigible.

"I had no idea you were so savage," she said, softly.

"I'm not savage," replied Freeman. "I am bored."

"Well, I don't know as I can blame you," said Grace, still more softly: she fancied he was referring to Miriam. "I don't much like Spanish mixtures myself."

"One has to take what one can get," said Freeman, referring to Don Miguel.

"But it's all right now," rejoined she, meaning that Freeman and herself were reconciled after their quarrel.

"If you are satisfied, I am," observed Freeman, too indifferent to care what she meant.

"Only, you mustn't take that poor young man too seriously," she went on: "these Mexicans are absurdly demonstrative, but they don't mean anything."

"He won't, if he values his skin," said Freeman, meaning that if Don Miguel attempted to interfere between himself and Miriam he would wring his neck.

"He won't, I promise you," said Grace, sparkling with pleasure.

"I don't quite see how you can help it," returned Freeman.

"I should hope I could manage a creature like that!" murmured she, smiling.

"Well," said Freeman, after a pause,—for Grace's seeming change of attitude puzzled him a little,—"I'm glad you look at it that way. I don't wish to be meddled with; that's all."

"You shan't be," she whispered; and then, just when they were approaching the point where their eyes might have been opened, in came General Trednoke. The group round the Golden Fleece broke up.

The general wore his riding-dress, and his bearing was animated, though he was covered with dust.

"I was wondering what had become of you all," he said, as the others gathered about him. "I have been taking a canter to the eastward. Kamaiakan said this morning that one of the boys had brought news of a cloud-burst in that direction. I rode far enough to ascertain that there has really been something of the kind, and I think it has affected the arroyo on the farther side of the little sierra. Now, I don't know how you gentlemen feel, but it occurred to me that it might be interesting to make up a little party of exploration to-morrow. Would you like to try it, Meschines?"

"To be sure I should!" the professor replied. "I imagine I can stand as much of the desert as you can! And I want to catch a sidewinder."

"Good! And you, Mr. Freeman?"

"It would suit me exactly," said the latter. "In fact, I had been intending to gratify my curiosity by making some such expedition on my own account."

"Ah!" said the general, eying him with some intentness. "Well, we may be able to show you something more curious than you anticipate.—And now, Senor de Mendoza, there is only you left. May we count on your company into the desert?"

But the Mexican, with a bow and a grimace, excused himself. Scientific curiosity was an unknown emotion to him; but he foresaw an opportunity to have Grace all to himself, and he meant to improve it. He also wished leisure to think over some plan for getting rid of Senor Freeman, in whom he scented a rival, and who, whether a rival or not, had behaved to him with a lack of consideration in the presence of ladies.

CHAPTER IV

General Trednoke's household went early to bed. As there was more accommodation in the old house than sufficed for its present inhabitants, it followed that each of them had a regal allowance of rooms. And when Grace Parsloe became one of the occupants, she was allotted two commodious apartments at the extremity of the left wing. They communicated, through long windows, with the veranda in front, and by means of doors with the passage, or hall, traversing the house from end to end. If, therefore, she happened to be sleepless, she might issue forth into the garden, and wander about there without let or hinderance until she was ready to accept the wooing of the god of dreams; or, if supernatural terrors daunted her, she could in a few seconds transfer herself and her fears to Miriam's chamber, which occupied the same position in the right wing that hers did in the left.

The night, as is customary in that climate, where the atmosphere is pure and evaporation rapid, was cool and still. By ten o'clock there was no sound to indicate that any person was awake; though, to an acute ear, the rise and fall of regular breathing, or even an occasional snore, might have given evidence of slumber. At the back of the house, the Indian retainers were lapped in silence. They were a harmless people,—somewhat disposed, perhaps, to small pilferings, in an amiable and loyal way, but incapable of anything seriously criminal. There were no locks on the doors, and most of them stood ajar. Tramps and burglars were unknown.

Miriam, having put on her night-dress, stood a few minutes at her window, gazing out on the soft darkness of the garden. All there was peacefulness and fragrance. The leaves of the plants hung motionless; the blossoms seemed to hush themselves to the enjoyment of their own sweetness. The sky was clear, but there was no moon. A beautiful planet, however, bright enough to cast a shadow, hung in the southwestern sky, and its mysterious light touched Miriam's face, and cast a dim rectangle of radiance on the white matting that carpeted the floor of her room. It was the planet Venus,—the star of love. Miriam thought it would be a pleasant place to live in. But one need not journey to Venus to find a world where love is the ruling passion. Circumstances over which she has no control may cause such a world to come into existence in a girl's heart.

She left the window at last, and got into bed, where she soon presented an image of perfect repose. Meanwhile, in a dark corner of the court-yard at the rear, a dark, pyramidal object abode without motion. It might have been taken for a heap of blankets piled up there. But if you examined it more narrowly you would have detected in it the vague outlines of a human figure, squatting on its haunches, with its head resting on its knees, and its arms clasped round them,— somewhat as figures sit in Egyptian hieroglyphics, or like Aztecan mummies in the tomb. So still was it, it might itself have been a mummy. But ever and anon a blinking of the narrow eyes in the bronze countenance told that it was no mummy, but a living creature. In fact, it was none other than the aged and austere Kamaiakan, who, for reasons best known to himself, chose to spend the hours usually devoted to rest in an attitude that no European or white American could have maintained with comfort longer than five minutes.

An hour—two hours—passed away. Then Kamaiakan noiselessly arose, peered about him cautiously for a few moments, and passed out of the court-yard through the open gate. He turned to the left, and, stealing beneath Miriam's windows, paused there for an instant and made certain gestures with his arms. Anon he continued his way to the garden, and was soon concealed by the thick shrubbery.

History requires us to follow him. The garden extended westward, and was quite a spacious enclosure: one not familiar with its winding paths might easily lose himself there on a dark night. But Kamaiakan knew where he was going, and the way thither. He now stalked along more swiftly, taking one turn after another, brushing aside the low-hanging boughs, and passing the loveliest flowers without a glance. He was as one preoccupied with momentous business. Presently he arrived at a small open space, remote and secluded. It was completely surrounded by tall shrubbery. In the centre was a basin of stone, evidently very ancient, filled to the brim with the clear water of a spring, which bubbled up from the bottom, and, overflowing by way of a gap in the edge, became a small rivulet, which stole away in the direction of the sea. Across the slightly undulating surface of the basin trembled the radiance of the star.

Kamaiakan knelt down beside it, and, bending over, gazed intently into the water. Presently he dipped his hands in it, and sprinkled shining drops over his own gaunt person, and over the ground in the vicinity of the spring. He made strange movements with his arms, bowed his head and erected it again, and traced curious figures on the ground

Julian Hawthorne

with his finger. It appeared as if the venerable Indian had solemnly lost his senses and had sought out this lonely spot to indulge the vagaries of his insanity. If so, his silence and deliberation afforded an example worthy of consideration by other lunatics.

Suddenly he ceased his performance, and held himself in a listening attitude. A light, measured sound was audible, accompanied by the rustling of leaves. It came nearer. There was a glimpse of whiteness through the interstices of the surrounding foliage, and then a slender figure, clad in close-fitting raiment, entered the little circle. It wore a sort of tunic, reaching half-way to the knees, and leggings of the same soft, grayish-white material. The head was covered with a sort of hood, which left only the face exposed; and this too might be covered by a species of veil or mask, which, however, was now fastened back on the headpiece, after the manner of a visor. The front of the tunic was embroidered with fantastic devices in gold thread, brightened here and there with precious stones; and other devices appeared on the hood. The face of this figure was pale and calm, with great dark eyes beneath black brows. The stature was no greater than that of a lad of fifteen, but the bearing was composed and dignified. The contours of the figure, however, even as seen by that dim light, were those of neither a boy nor a man. The wearer of the tunic was a girl, just rounding into womanhood, and the face was the face of Miriam.

Yet it was not by this name that Kamaiakan addressed her. After making a deep obeisance, touching his hand to her foot and then to his own forehead and breast, he said, in a language that was neither Spanish nor such as the modern Indians of Mexico use,—

"Welcome, Semitzin! May this night be the beginning of

high things!"

"I am ready," replied the other, in a soft and low voice, but with a certain stateliness of utterance unlike the usual manner of General Trednoke's daughter: "I was glad to hear you call, and to see again the stars and the earth. Have you anything to tell?"

"There are events which may turn to our harm, most revered princess. The master of this house—"

"Why do you not call him my father, Kamaiakan?" interposed the other. "He is indeed the father of this mortal body which I wear, which (as you tell me) bears the name of Miriam. Besides, are not Miriam and I united by the thread of descent?"

"Something of the spirit that is you dwells in her also," said the Indian.

"And does she know of it?"

"At times, my princess; but only as one remembers a dream."

"I wish I might converse with her and instruct her in the truth," said the princess. "And she, in turn, might speak to me of things that perplex me. I live and move in this mortal world, and yet (you tell me) three centuries have passed since what is called my death. To me it seems as if I had but slept through a night, and were awake again. Nor can I tell what has happened—what my life and thoughts have been— during this long lapse of time. Yet it must be that I live another life: I cannot rest in extinction. Three times you have called me forth; yet whence I come hither, or whither I return, is unknown to me."

Julian Hawthorne

"There is a memory of the spirit," replied Kamaiakan, "and a memory of the body. They are separate, and cannot communicate with each other. Such is the law."

"Yet I remember, as if it were yesterday, the things that were done when Montezuma was king. And well do I remember you, Kamaiakan!"

"It is true I live again, princess, though not in the flesh and bones that died with you in the past. But in the old days I was acquainted with mysteries, and learned the secrets of the world of spirits; and this science still remained with me after the change, so that I was able to know that I was I, and that you could be recalled to speak with me through the tongue of Miriam. But there are some things that I do not know; and it is for that I have been bold to summon you."

"What can I tell you that can be of use to you in this present life, Kamaiakan, when all whom we knew and loved are gone?"

"To you only, Semitzin, is known the place of concealment of the treasure which, in the old times, you and I hid in the desert. I indeed remember the event, and somewhat of the region of the hiding; but I cannot put my hand upon the very spot. I have tried to discover it; but when I approach it my mind becomes confused between the present and the past, and I am lost."

"I remember it well," said Semitzin. "We rode across the desert, carrying the treasure on mules. The air was still, and the heat very heavy. The desert descended in a great hollow: you told me it was where, in former days, the ocean had been. At last there were rocky hills before us; we rode towards a great rock shaped like the pyramid on which the sacrifices were held in Tenochtitlan. We passed round its base, and entered a deep and narrow valley, that seemed to have been ploughed out of the heart of the earth and to descend into it. Then—But what is it you wish to do with this treasure, Kamaiakan?"

"It belongs to your race, princess, and was hidden that the murderers of Montezuma might not seize it. I was bound by an oath, after the peril was past, to restore it to the rightful owners. But our country remained under the rule of the conquerors; and my life went out. But now the conquerors have been conquered in their turn, and Miriam is the last inheritor of your blood. When I have delivered to her this trust, my work will be done, and I can return to the world which you inhabit. The time is come; and only by your help can the restitution be made."

"Was there, then, a time fixed?"

"The stars tell me so. And other events make it certain that there must be no delay. The general has it in mind to discover the gates through which the waters under-ground may arise and again form the sea which flowed hereabouts in the ancient times. Now, this sea will fill the ravine in which the treasure lies, and make it forever unattainable. A youth has also come here who is skilled in the sciences, and whom the general will ask to help him in the thing he is to attempt."

"Who is this youth?" asked Semitzin.

"He is of the new people who inherit this land: his name is Freeman."

"There is something in me—I know not what—that seems to tell me I have been near such a one. Can it be so?"

"The other self, who now sleeps, knows of him," replied the

ancient Indian. "He is a well-looking youth, and I think he has a desire towards her we call Miriam."

"And does she love him?" inquired the princess.

"A maiden's heart is a riddle, even to herself," said Kamaiakan.

"But there is a sympathy that makes me feel her heart in my own," rejoined Semitzin. "Love is a thing that pierces through time, and through barriers which separate the mind and memory of the past from the present. I—as you know, Kamaiakan—was never wedded; the fate of our people, and my early end, kept that from me. But the thought of that youth is here,"—she put her hand on her bosom,—"and it seems to me that, were we to meet, I should know him. Perhaps, were that to be, Miriam and I might thus come to be aware of each other, and live henceforth one life."

"Such matters are beyond my knowledge," said the Indian, shaking his head. "The gods know what will be. It is for us, now, to regain the treasure. Are you willing, my princess, to accompany me thither?"

"I am ready. Shall it be now?"

"Not now, but soon. I will call you when the moment comes. The place is but a ride of two or three hours from here. None must know of our departure, for there are some here whom I do not trust. We must go by night. You will wear the garments you now have on, without which all might miscarry."

"How can the garments affect the result, Kamaiakan?"

"A powerful spell is laid upon them, princess. Moreover, the characters wrought upon them, with gold thread and jewels, are mystical, and the substance of the garment itself has a virtue to preserve the wearer from evil. It is the same that was worn by you when the treasure was hidden; and it may be, Semitzin, that without its magic aid your spirit could not know itself in this world as now it can."

As he spoke the last words, a low sound, wandering and muttering with an inward note, came palpitating on their ears through the night air. It seemed to approach from no direction that could be identified, yet it was at first remote, and then came nearer, and in a moment trembled around them, and shivered in the solid earth beneath their feet; and in another instant it had passed on, and was subdued slowly into silence in the shadowy distance. No one who has once heard that sound can mistake it for any other, or ever can forget it. The air had suddenly become close and tense; and now a long breeze swept like a sigh through the garden, dying away in a long-drawn wail; and out of the west came a hollow murmur, like that of a mighty wave breaking upon the shore of the ocean.

"The earthquake!" whispered Kamaiakan, rising to his feet. And then he pointed to the stone basin. "Look! the spring!"

"It is gone!" exclaimed Semitzin.

And, in truth, the water, with a strange, sucking noise, disappeared through the bottom of the basin, leaving the glistening cavity which had held it, green with slimy water-weed, empty.

"The time is near, indeed!" muttered the Indian. "The second shock may cause the waters from which this spring came to rise as no living man has seen them rise, and make the sea return, and the treasure be lost. In a few days all may be over. But you, princess, must vanish: though the shock was but slight, some one might be awakened; and were you to be discovered, our plans might go wrong."

"Must I depart so soon?" said Semitzin, regretfully. "The earth is beautiful, Kamaiakan: the smell of the flowers is sweet, and the stars in the sky are bright. To feel myself alive, to breathe, to walk, to see, are sweet. Perhaps I have no other conscious life than this. I would like to remain as I am: I would like to see the sun shine, and to hear the birds sing, and to see the men and women who live in this age. Is there no way of keeping me here?"

"I cannot tell; it may be,—but it must not be now, Semitzin," the old man replied, with a troubled look. "The ways of the gods are not our ways. She whose body you inhabit—she has her life to live."

"But is that girl more worthy to live than I? You have called me into being again: you have made me know how pleasant this world is. Miriam sleeps: she need never know; she need never awake again. You were faithful to me in the old time: have you more care for her than for me? I feel all the power and thirst of youth in me: the gods did not let me live out my life: may they not intend that I shall take it up again now? Besides, I wear Miriam's body: could I not seem to others to be Miriam indeed? How could they guess the truth?"

"I will think of what you say, princess," said Kamaiakan. "Something may perhaps be done; but it must be done gradually: you would need much instruction in the ways of the new world before you could safely enter into its life. Leave that to me. I am loyal as ever: is it not to fulfil the oath made to you that I am here? and what would Miriam be to me, were she not your inheritor? Be satisfied for the present: in a few days we will meet and speak again."

"The power is yours, Kamaiakan: it is well to argue, when with a word you can banish me forever! Yet what if I were to say that, unless you consent to the thing I desire, I will not show you where the treasure lies?"

"Princess Semitzin!" exclaimed the Indian, "remember that it is not against me, but against the gods, that you would contend. The gods know that I have no care for treasure. But they will not forgive a broken oath; and they will not hold that one guiltless through whom it is brought to naught?"

"Well, we shall meet again," answered Semitzin, after a pause. "But do you remember that you, too, are not free from responsibility in this matter. You have called me back: see to it that you do me justice." She waved her hands with a gesture of adieu, turned, and left the enclosure. Kamaiakan sank down again beside the empty bowl of the fountain.

Semitzin returned along the path by which she had come, towards the house. As she turned round one of the corners, she saw a man's figure before her, strolling slowly along in the same direction in which she was going. In a few moments he heard her light footfall, and, facing about, confronted her. She continued to advance until she was within arm's reach of him: then she paused, and gazed steadfastly in his face. He was the first human being, save Kamaiakan, that she had seen since her eyes closed upon the world of Tenochtitlan, three hundred years before.

The young man looked upon her with manifest surprise. It was too dark to distinguish anything clearly, but it did not take him long to surmise that the figure was that of a woman, and her countenance, though changed in aspect by the head-dress she were, yet had features which, he knew, he had seen before. But could it be Miriam Trednoke who was abroad at such an hour and in such a costume? He did not recognize the Golden Fleece, but it was evident enough that she was clad as women are not.

Before he could think of anything to say to her, she smiled, and uttered some words in a soft, flowing language with which he was entirely unacquainted. The next moment she had glided past him, and was out of sight round the curve of the path, leaving him in a state of perplexity not altogether gratifying.

"What the deuce can it mean?" he muttered to himself. "I can't be mistaken about its being Miriam. And yet she didn't look at me as if she recognized me. What can she be doing out here at midnight? I suppose it's none of my business: in fact, she might very reasonably ask the same question of me. And if I were to tell her that I had only ridden over to spend a sentimental hour beneath her window, what would she say? If she answered in the same lingo she used just now, I should be as wise as before. After all, it may have been somebody else. The image in my mind projected itself on her countenance. I certainly must be in love! I almost wish I'd never come here. This complication about the general's irrigating scheme makes it awkward. I'm bound not to explain things to him; and yet, if I don't, and he discovers (as he can't help doing) what I am here for, nothing will persuade him that I haven't been playing a double game; and that would not be a promising preliminary towards becoming a member of his family. If Miriam were only Grace, now, it would be plain sailing. Hello! who's this? Senor Don Miguel, as I'm a sinner! What is he up to, pray? Can this be the explanation of Miriam's escapade? I have a strong desire to blow a hole through that fellow!—Buenas noches, Senor de Mendoza! I am enchanted to have the unexpected honor of meeting you."

Senor de Mendoza turned round, disagreeably startled. It is only fair to explain that he had not come hither with any lover- like designs towards Miriam. Grace was the magnet that had drawn his steps to the Trednokes' garden, and the truth is that that enterprising young lady was not without a suspicion that he might turn up. Could this information have been imparted to Freeman, it would have saved much trouble; but, as it was, not only did he jump to the conclusion that Don Miguel was his rival (and, seemingly, a not unsuccessful one), but a similar misgiving as to Freeman's purposes towards Grace found its way into the heart of the Spaniard. It was a most perverse trick of fate.

The two men contemplated each other, each after his own fashion: Don Miguel pale, glaring, bristling; Freeman smiling, insolent, hectoring.

"Why are you here, senor?" demanded the former, at length.

"Partly, senor, because such is my pleasure. Partly, to inform you that your presence here offends me, and to humbly request you to be off."

"Senor, this is an impertinence."

"Senor, one is not impertinent to prowling greasers. One admonishes them, and, if they do not obey, one chastises them."

"Do you talk of chastising Don Miguel de Mendoza? Senor, I will wash out that insult with your blood!"

"Excellent! It is at your service for the taking. But, lest we disturb the repose of our friends yonder, let us seek a more convenient spot. I noticed a very pretty little glade on the right as I rode over here. You are armed? Good! we will have this little affair adjusted within half an hour. Yonder star—the planet of love, senor—shall see fair play. Andamos!"

CHAPTER V

Having mounted their steeds, the two sanguinary young gentlemen rode onwards, side by side, but in silence; for the souls of those who have resolved to slay each other find small delight in vain conversation. Moreover, there is that in the conscious proximity of death which stimulates to thought much more than to speech. But Freeman preserved an outward demeanor of complacent calm, as one who doubts not, nor dreads, the issue; and, indeed, this was not the first time by many that he had taken his life in his hand and brought it unscathed through dangers. Don Miguel, on the other hand, was troubled in spirit, and uneasy in the flesh. He was one soon hot and soon cold; and this long ride to the decisive event went much against his stomach. If the conflict had taken place there in the garden, while the fire of the insult was yet scorching him, he could have fought it out with good will; but now the night air seemed chiller and chiller, and its frigidity crept into his nerves: he doubted of the steadiness of his aim, bethought himself that the darkness was detrimental to accurate shooting, and wondered whether Senor Freeman would think it necessary to fight across a handkerchief. He could not help regretting, too, that the quarrel had not been occasioned by some more definite and satisfactory provocation,—something which merely to think of would steel the heart to irrevocable murderousness. But no blow had passed; even the words, though bitter to swallow, had been wrapt in the phrases of courtesy; and perhaps the whole affair was the result of some misapprehension. He stole a look at the face of his companion; and the latter's air of confident and cheerful serenity made him feel worse than ever. Was he being brought out here to be butchered for nothing,—he, Don Miguel de Mendoza, who had looked forward to many pleasures in this life? It was too bad. It was true, the fortune of war might turn the other way; but Don Miguel was aware of a sensation in his bones which made this hope weak.

At length Freeman drew rein and glanced around him. They were in a lonely and—Don Miguel thought—a most desolate and unattractive spot. An open space of about half an acre was bounded on one side by a growth of wild mustard, whose slender stalks rose to more than the height of a man's head. On the other side was a grove of live-oak; and in front, the ground fell away in a rugged, bush-grown declivity.

"It strikes me that this is just about what we want," remarked Freeman, in his full, cheerful tones. "We are half a mile from the road; the ground is fairly level; and there's no possibility of our being disturbed. I was thinking, this afternoon, as I passed through here, what an ideal spot it was for just such a little affair as you and I are bent on. But I didn't venture to anticipate such speedy good fortune as your obliging condescension has brought to pass, Don Miguel."

"Caramba!" muttered the senor, shivering. He might have said more, but was unwilling to trust his voice, or to waste nervous energy.

Meanwhile, Freeman had dismounted, and was tethering his horse. It occurred to the senor that it would be easy to pull his gun, send a bullet through his companion, and gallop away. He did not yield to this temptation, partly from

Julian Hawthorne

traditional feeling that it would not be suitable conduct for a De Mendoza, partly because he might miss the shot or only inflict a wound, and partly because such deeds demand a nerve which, at that moment, was not altogether at his command. Instead, he slowly dismounted himself, and wondered whether it would ever be vouchsafed him to sit in that saddle again.

Freeman now produced his revolver, a handsome, silver-mounted weapon, that looked business-like. "What sort of a machine is yours?" he inquired, pleasantly. "You can take your choice. I'm not particular, but I can recommend this as a sure thing, if you would like to try it. It never misses at twenty paces."

"Twenty paces?" repeated Don Miguel, with a faint gleam of hope.

"Of course we won't have any twenty paces to-night, "added Freeman, with a laugh. "I thought it might be a good plan to start at, say, fifteen, and advance firing. In that way, one or other of us will be certain to do something sooner or later. Would that arrangement be agreeable to Senor de Mendoza?"

"Valga me Dios! I am content," said the latter, fetching a deep breath, and setting his teeth. "I will keep my weapon."

"Muy buen," returned the American. "So now let us take our ground: that is, if you are quite ready?"

Accordingly they selected their stations, facing respectively about north and south, with the planet of love between them, as it were. "Oblige me by giving the word, senor," said Freeman, cocking his weapon.

But Don Miguel was staring with perturbed visage at something behind his antagonist. "Santa Maria!" he faltered, "what is yonder? It is a spirit!"

Freeman had his wits about him, and perhaps entertained a not too high opinion of Mexican fair play. So, before turning round, he advanced till he was alongside his companion. Then he looked, and saw something which was certainly enigmatic.

Among the wild-mustard plants there appeared a moving luminosity, having an irregular, dancing motion, as of a will-o'-the- wisp singularly agitated. Sometimes it uplifted itself on high, then plunged downwards, and again jerked itself from side to side; occasionally it would quite vanish for an instant. Accompanying this manifestation there was a clawing and reaching of shadowy arms: altogether, it was as if some titanic spectral grasshopper, with a heart of fire, were writhing and kicking in convulsions of phantom agony. Such an apparition, in an hour and a place so lonely, might stagger a less superstitious soul than that of Don Miguel de Mendoza.

Freeman gazed at it for a moment in silence. It mystified him, and then irritated him. When one is bent heart and soul upon an important enterprise, any interruption is an annoy-ance. Perhaps there was in the young American's nature just enough remains of belief in witches and hobgoblins to make him feel warranted in resorting to extreme measures. At any rate, he lifted his revolver, and fired.

It was a long shot for a revolver: nevertheless it took effect. The luminous object disappeared with a faint explosive sound, followed by a shout unmistakably human. The long stems of the wild mustard swayed and parted, and out sprang a figure, which ran straight towards the two young men.

Hereupon, Don Miguel, hissing out an appeal to the Virgin and the saints, turned and fled.

Meanwhile, the mysterious figure continued its onward career; and Freeman once more levelled his weapon,—when a voice, which gave him such a start of surprise as well-nigh caused him to pull the trigger for sheer lack of self-command, called out, "Why, you abominable young villain! What the mischief do you mean? Do you want to be hanged?"

"Professor Meschines!" faltered Freeman.

It was indeed that worthy personage, and he was on fire with wrath. He held in one hand a shattered lantern mounted on the end of a pole, and in the other a long- handled net of gauze, such as entomologists use to catch moths withal. Under his left arm was slung a brown japanned case, in which he presumably deposited the spoils of his skill. Freeman's shot had not only smashed and extinguished the lantern which served as bait for the game, but had also given the professor a disagreeable reminder that the tenure of human life is as precarious as that of the silly moth which allows itself to be lured to destruction by shining promises of bliss.

"Upon my soul, professor, I am very sorry," said Freeman. "You have no idea how formidable you looked; and you could hardly expect me to imagine that you would be abroad at such an hour—"

"And why not, I should like to know?" shouted the professor, towering with indignation. "Was I doing anything to be ashamed of? And what are you doing here, pray, with loaded revolvers in your hands?—Hallo! who's this?" he exclaimed, as Don Miguel advanced doubtfully out of the gloom. "Senor de Mendoza, as I'm a sinner! and armed, too! Well, really! Are you two out on a murdering expedition?—Oho!" he went on, in a changed tone, glancing keenly from one to another: "methinks I see the bottom of this mystery. You have ridden forth, like the champions of romance, to do doughty deeds upon each other!—Is it not so, Don Miguel?" he demanded, turning his fierce spectacles suddenly on that young man.

Don Miguel, ignoring a secret gesture from Freeman, admitted that he had been on the point of expunging the latter from this mortal sphere.

The professor chuckled sarcastically. "I see! Blood! Wounded honor! The code!—But, by the way, I don't see your seconds! Where are your seconds?"

"My dear sir," said Freeman, "I assure you it's all a mistake. We just happened to meet at the gen—er—happened to meet, and were riding home together—"

"Now, listen to me, Harvey," the professor interrupted, holding up an expository finger. "You have known me since some ten years, I think; and I have known you. You were a clever boy in your studies; but it was your foible to fancy yourself cleverer than you were. Acting under that delusion, you pitted yourself against me on one or two occasions; and I leave it to your candid recollection whether you or I had the best of the encounter. You call yourself a man, now; but I make bold to say that the—discrepancy, let us call it— between you and me remains as conspicuous as ever it was. I see through you, sir, much more clearly than, by this light, I can see you. I am fond of you, Harvey; but I feel nothing but contempt for your present attitude. In the first place, conscious as you are of your skill with that weapon, you know that this affair—even had seconds been present—

would have been, not a duel, but an assassination. You acted like a coward!—I say it, sir, like a coward!— and I hope you may live to be as much ashamed of yourself as I am now ashamed for you. Secondly, your conduct, considered in its relations to—to certain persons whom I will not name, is that of a boor and a blackguard. Suppose you had accomplished the cowardly murder—the cowardly murder, I said, sir—that you were bent upon to-night. Do you think that would be a grateful and acceptable return for the courtesy and confidence that have been shown you in that house?—a house, sir, to which I myself introduced you, under the mistaken belief that you were a gentleman, or, at least, could feign gentlemanly behavior! But I won't—my feelings won't allow me to enlarge further upon this point. But allow me to add, in the third place, that you have shown yourself a purblind donkey. Actually, you haven't sense enough to know the difference between those who pull with you and those who pull against you. Now, I happen to know—to know, do you hear?—that had you succeeded in what you were just about to attempt, you would have removed your surest ally,—the surest, because his interests prompt him to favor yours. You pick out the one man who was doing his best to clear the obstacle out of your path, and what do you do?—Thank him?—Not you! You plot to kill him! But even had he been, as you in your stupidity imagined, your rival, do you think the course you adopted would have promoted your advantage? Let me tell you, sir, that you don't know the kind of people you are dealing with. You would never have been permitted to cross their threshold again. And you may take my word for it, if ever you venture to recur to any such folly, I will see to it that you receive your deserts.—Well, I think we understand each other, now?"

Freeman's emotions had undergone several variations during the course of the mighty professor's harangue. But he had ended by admitting the force of the argument; and the reminiscences of college lecturings aroused by the incident had tickled his sense of humor and quenched his anger. He looked at the professor with a sparkle of laughter in his eyes.

"I have done very wrong, sir," he said, "and I'm very sorry for it. If you won't give me any bad marks this time, I'll promise to be good in future."

"Ah! very smooth! To begin with, suppose you ask pardon of Senor Don Miguel de Mendoza for the affront you have put upon him."

To a soul really fearless, even an apology has no terrors. Moreover, Freeman's night ride with Don Miguel, though brief in time, had sufficed to give him the measure of the Mexican's character; and he respected it so little that he could no longer take the man seriously, or be sincerely angry with him. The professor's assurance as to Don Miguel's inoffensiveness had also its weight; and it was therefore with a quite royal gesture of amicable condescension that Freeman turned upon his late antagonist and held out his hand.

"Senor Don Miguel de Mendoza," said he, "I humbly tender you my apologies and crave your pardon. My conduct has been inexcusable; I beg you to excuse it. I deserve your reprobation; I entreat the favor of your friendship. Senor, between men of honor, a misunderstanding is a misunderstanding, and an apology is an apology. I lament the existence of the first; the professor, here, is witness that I lay the second at your feet. May I hope to receive your hand as a pledge that you restore me to the privilege of your good will?"

Now, Don Miguel's soul had been grievously exercised that night: he had been insulted, he had shivered beneath the shadow of death, he had been a prey to superstitious terrors, and he had been utterly perplexed by the professor's eloquent address, whereof (as it was delivered in good American, and with a rapidity of utterance born of strong feeling) he had comprehended not a word, and the unexpected effect of which upon his late adversary he was at a loss to understand. Although, therefore, he had no stomach for battle, he was oppressed by a misgiving lest the whole transaction had been in some way planned to expose him to ridicule; and for this reason he was disposed to treat Freeman's peaceful overtures with suspicion. His heart did not respond to those overtures, but neither was it stout enough to enable him to reject them explicitly. Accordingly, he adopted that middle course which, in spite of the proverb, is not seldom the least expedient. He disregarded the proffered hand, bowed very stiffly, and, saying, "Senor, I am satisfied," stalked off with all the rigidity of one in whose veins flows the sangre azul of Old Castile. Freeman smiled superior upon his retreat, and then, producing a cigar-case, proceeded to light up with the professor. In this fragrant and friendly cloud we will leave them, and return for a few minutes to the house of General Trednoke.

It will be remembered that something was said of Grace being privy to the nocturnal advances of Senor de Mendoza. We are not to suppose that this implies in her anything worse than an aptness to indulge in romantic adventure: the young lady enjoyed the mystery of romance, and knew that serenades, and whisperings over star-lit balconies, were proper to this latitude. It may be open to question whether she really was much interested in De Mendoza, save as he was a type of the adoring Spaniard. That the scene required: she could imagine him (for the time-being) to be the Cid of ancient legend, and she herself would enact a role of corresponding elevation. Grace would doubtless have prospered better had she been content with one adorer at a time; but, while turning to a new love, she was by no means disposed to loosen the chains of a former one; and, though herself as jealous as is a tiger-cat of her young, she could never recognize the propriety of a similar passion on the part of her victims. She had been indignant at Freeman's apparent infidelity with Miriam; but when she had (as she imagined) discovered her mistake, she had listened with a heart at ease to the protestations of Don Miguel. She had parted from him that evening with a half expressed understanding that he was to reappear beneath her window before day-light; and she had pictured to herself a charming balcony-scene, such as she had beheld in Italian opera. Accordingly, she had attired herself in a becoming negligee, and had spent the fore part of the night somewhat restlessly, occasionally emerging on the veranda and gazing down into the perfumed gloom of the garden. At length she fancied that she heard footsteps. Whose could they be, unless Don Miguel's? Grace retreated within her window to await developments. Don Miguel did not appear; but presently she descried a phantom-like figure ascending the flight of steps to the veranda. Could that be he? If so, he was bolder in his wooing than Grace had been prepared for. But surely that was a strange costume that he wore; nor did the unconscious harmony of the gait at all resemble the senor's self-conscious strut. And whither was he going?

It was but too evident that he was going straight to the room occupied by Miriam!

This was too much for Grace's equanimity. She stepped out of her window, and flitted with noiseless step along the veranda. The figure that she pursued entered the door of the house, and passed into the corridor traversing the wing. Grace was in time to see it cross the threshold of Miriam's door, which stood ajar. She stole to the door, and peeped in. There was the figure; but of Miriam there was no trace.

The figure slowly unfastened and threw back the hood which covered its head, at the same time turning round, so that its countenance was revealed. A torrent of black hair fell down over its shoulders. Grace uttered an involuntary exclamation. It was Miriam herself!

The two gazed at each other a moment in silence. "Goodness me, dear!" said Grace at last, in a faint voice, "how you have frightened me! I saw you go in, in that dress, and I thought you were a man! How my heart beats! What is the matter?"

"This is strange!" murmured the other, after a pause. "I never heard such words; and yet I seem to understand, and even to speak them. It must be a dream. What are you?"

"Why, Miriam, dear! don't you know Grace?"

"Oh! you think me Miriam. No; not yet!" She raised her hands, and pressed her fingers against her temples. "But I feel her—I feel her coming! Not yet, Kamaiakan! not so soon!—Do you know him?" she suddenly asked, throwing back her hair, and fixing an eager gaze on Grace.

"Know who? Kamaiakan? Why, yes—"

"No, not him! The youth,—the blue-eyed,—the fair beard above his lips—"

"What are you talking about? Not Harvey Freeman!"

"Harvey Freeman! Ah, how sweet a name! Harvey Freeman! I shall know it now!—Tell him," she went on, laying her hand majestically upon Grace's shoulder, and speaking with an impressive earnestness, "that Semitzin loves him!"

"Semitzin?" repeated Grace, puzzled, and beginning to feel scared.

"Semitzin!" the other said, pointing to her own heart. "She loves him: not as the child Miriam loves, but with the heart and soul of a mighty princess. When he knows Semitzin, he will think of Miriam no more."

"But who is Semitzin?" inquired Grace, with a fearful curiosity.

"The Princess of Tenochtitlan, and the guardian of the great treasure, "was the reply.

"Good gracious! what treasure?"

"The treasure of gold and precious stones hidden in the gorge of the desert hills. None knows the place of it but I; and I will give it to none but him I love."

"But you said that . . . Really, my dear, I don't understand a bit! As for Mr. Freeman, he may care for Semitzin, for aught I know; but, I must confess, I think you're mistaken in supposing he's in love with you,—if that is what you mean. I met him before you did, you know; and if I were to tell you all that we—"

"What are you or Miriam to me?—Ah! she comes!—The treasure—by the turning of the white pyramid—six hundred paces—on the right—the arch—" Her voice died away. She covered her face with her hands, and trembled violently. Slowly she let them fall, and stared around her. "Grace, is it you? Has anything happened? How came I like this? What is it?"

"Well, if you don't know, I'm afraid I can't tell you. I had begun to think you had gone mad. It must be either that or somnambulism. Who is Semitzin?"

"Semitzin? I never heard of him."

"It isn't a man: it's a princess. And the treasure?"

"Am I asleep or awake? What are you saying?"

"The white pyramid, you know—"

"Don't make game of me, Grace. If I have done anything—"

"My dear, don't ask me! I tell you frankly, I'm nonplussed. You were somebody else a minute ago. . . . The truth is, of course, you've been dreaming awake. Has any one else seen you beside me?"

"Have I been out of my room?" asked Miriam, in dismay.

"You must have been, I should think, to get that costume. Well, the best plan will be, I suppose, to say nothing about it to anybody. It shall be our secret, dear. If I were you, I would have one of the women sleep in your room, in case you got restless again. It's just an attack of nervousness, probably,— having so many strangers in the house, all of a sudden. Now you must go to bed and get to sleep: it's awfully late, and there'll be ever so much going on to- morrow."

Grace herself slept little that night. She could not decide what to make of this adventure. Nowadays we are provided with a name for the peculiar psychical state which Miriam was undergoing, and with abundant instances and illustrations; but we perhaps know what it is no more than we did twenty-five or thirty years ago. Grace's first idea had been that Miriam was demented; then she thought she was playing a part; then she did not know what to think; and finally she came to the conclusion that it was best to quietly await further developments. She would keep an eye on Freeman as well as on Miriam; something, too, might be gathered from Don Miguel; and then there was that talk about a treasure. Was that all the fabric of a dream, or was there truth at the bottom of it? She had heard something said about a treasure in the course of the general conversation the day before. If there really was a treasure, why might not she have a hand in the discovery of it? Miriam, in her abnormal state, had let fall some topographical hints that might prove useful. Well, she would work out the problem, sooner or later. To-morrow, when the others had gone off on their expedition, she would have ample leisure to sound Don Miguel, and, if he proved communicative and available, who could tell what might happen? But how very odd it all was! Who was Semitzin?

While asking herself this question, Grace fell asleep; and by the time the summons to breakfast came, she had passed through thrilling adventures enough to occupy a new Scheherazade at least three years in the telling of them.

CHAPTER VI

By nine o'clock in the morning, Professor Meschines and Harvey Freeman had ridden up to the general's ranch, equipped for the expedition. The general's preparations were not yet quite completed. A couple of mules were being loaded with the necessary outfit. It was proposed to be out two days, camping in the open during the intervening night. It was necessary to take water as well as solid provisions. Leaving their horses in the care of a couple of stable-boys, Meschines and Freeman mounted the veranda, and were there greeted by General Trednoke.

"I'm afraid we'll have a hot ride of it," he observed. "The atmosphere is rather oppressive. Kamaiakan tells me there was a touch of earthquake last night."

"I thought I noticed some disturbance,—" returned the professor, with a stealthy side-glance at Freeman,—"something in the nature of an explosion."

"Earthquakes are common in this region, aren't they?" Freeman said.

"They have made it what it is, and may unmake it again," replied the general. "The earthquake is the father of the desert, as the Indians say; and it may some day become the father of a more genial offspring. Veremos!"

"How are the young ladies?" inquired Freeman.

"Miriam has a little headache, I believe; and I thought Miss Parsloe was looking a trifle pale this morning. But you must see for yourself. Here they come."

Grace, who was a little taller than Miriam, had thrown one arm round that young lady's waist, with a view, perhaps, to forming a picture in which she should not be the secondary figure. In fact, they were both of them very pretty; but Freeman had become blind to any beauty but Miriam's. Moreover, he was resolved to have some private conversation with her during the few minutes that were available. A conversation with the professor, and some meditations of his own, had suggested to him a line of attack upon Grace.

"I'm afraid you were disturbed by the earthquake last night?" he said to her.

"An earthquake? Why should you think so?"

"You look as if you had passed a restless night. I saw Senor de Mendoza this morning. He seems to have had a restless time of it, too. But he is a romantic person, and probably, if an earthquake did not make him sleepless, something else might." He looked at her a moment, and then added, with a smile, "But perhaps this is not news to you?"

"He didn't come—I didn't see him," returned Grace, wishing, ere the words had left her lips, that she had kept her mouth shut. Freeman continued to smile. How much did he know? She felt that it might be inexpedient to continue the conversation. Casting about for a pretext for retreat, her eyes fell upon Meschines.

"Oh, there's the dear professor! I must speak to him a moment," she exclaimed, vivaciously; and she slipped her arm from Miriam's waist, and was off, leaving Freeman in possession of the field, and of the monopoly of Miriam's society.

"Miss Trednoke," said he, gravely, "I have something to tell you, in order to clear myself from a possible misunderstanding. It may happen that I shall need your vindication with your father. Will you give it?"

"What vindication do you need, that I can give?" asked she, opening her dark eyes upon him questioningly.

"That's what I wish to explain. I am in a difficult position. Would you mind stepping down into the garden? It won't take a minute."

Curiosity, if not especially feminine, is at least human. Miriam descended the steps, Freeman beside her. They strolled down the path, amidst the flowers.

"You said, yesterday," he began, "that I would say one thing and be another. Now I am going to tell you what I am. And afterwards I'll tell you why I tell it. In the first place, you know, I'm a civil engineer, and that includes, in my case, a good deal of knowledge about geology and things of that sort. I have sometimes been commissioned to make geological surveys for Eastern capitalists. Lately I've been canal-digging on the Isthmus; but the other day I got a notification from some men in Boston and New York to come out here on a secret mission."

"Secret, Mr. Freeman?"

"Yes: you will understand directly. These men had heard

enough about the desert valleys of this region to lead them to think that it might be reclaimed and so be made very valuable. Such lands can be bought now for next to nothing; but, if the theories that control these capitalists are correct, they could afterwards be sold at a profit of thousands per cent. So it's indispensable that the object of my being here should remain unknown; otherwise, other persons might step in and anticipate the designs of this company."

"If those are your orders, why do you speak to me?"

"There's a reason for doing it that outweighs the reasons against it. I trust you with the secret: yet I don't mean to bind you to secrecy. You will have a perfect right to tell it: the only result would be that I should be discredited with my employers; and there is nothing to warrant me in supposing that you would be deterred by that."

"I don't ask to know your secret: I think you had better say no more."

Freeman shook his head. "I must speak," said he. "I don't care what becomes of me, so long as I stand right in your opinion,—your father's and yours. I am here to find out whether this desert can be flooded,—irrigated,—whether it's possible, by any means, to bring water upon it. If my report is favorable, the company will purchase hundreds, or thousands, of square miles, and, incidentally, my own fortune will be made."

"Why, that's the very thing—" She stopped.

"The very thing your father had thought of! Yes, so I imagined, though he has not told me so in so many words. So I'm in the position of surreptitiously taking away the prospective fortune of a man whom I respect and honor, and who treats me as a friend."

Miriam walked on some steps in silence. "It is no fault of yours," she said at last. "You owe us nothing. You must carry out your orders."

"Yes; but what is to prevent your father from thinking that I stole his idea and then used it against him?"

"You can tell him the truth: he could not complain; and why should you care if he did? I know that men separate business from—from other things."

They had now come to the little enclosed space where the fountain basin was; and by tacit consent they seated themselves upon it. Miriam gave an exclamation of surprise. "The water is gone!" she said. "How strange!"

"Perhaps it has gone to meet us at our rendezvous in the desert.—No: if I tell your father, I should be unfaithful to my employers. But there's another alternative: I can resign my appointment, and let my place be taken by another."

"And give up your chance of a fortune? You mustn't do that."

"What is it to you what becomes of me?"

"I wish nothing but good to come to you," said she, in a low voice.

"I have never wanted to have a fortune until now. And I must tell you the reason of that, too. A man without a fortune does very well by himself. He can knock about, and live from hand to mouth. But when he wants to live for somebody else,—even if he has only a very faint hope of getting the opportunity of doing it,—then he must have some settled means of livelihood to justify him. So I say I am in a difficult position. For if I give this up, I must go away; and if I go away, I must give up even the little hope I have."

"Don't go away," said Miriam, after a pause.

"Do you know what you are saying?" He hesitated a moment, looking at her as she looked down at the empty basin. "My hope was that you might love me; for I love you, to be my wife."

The color slowly rose in Miriam's face: at length she hid it in her hands. "Oh, what is it?" she said, almost in a whisper. "I have known you only three days. But it seems as if I must have known you before. There is something in me that is not like myself. But it is the deepest thing in me; and it loves you: yes, I love you!"

Her hands left her face, and there was a light in her eyes which made Freeman, in the midst of his rejoicing, feel humble and unworthy. He felt himself in contact with something pure and sacred. At the same moment, the recollection recurred to him of the figure he had seen the night before, with the features of Miriam. Was it she indeed? Was this she? To doubt the identity of the individual is to lose one's footing on the solid earth. For the first time it occurred to him that this doubt might affect Miriam herself. Was she obscurely conscious of two states of being in herself, and did she therefore fear to trust her own impulses? But, again, love is the master-passion; its fire fuses all things, and gives them unity. Would not this love that they confessed for each other burn away all that was abnormal and enigmatic, and leave only the unerring human heart, that knows its own and takes it? These reflections passed through Freeman's mind in an instant of time. But he was no

Julian Hawthorne

metaphysician, and he obeyed the sane and wholesome instinct which has ever been man's surest and safest guide through the mysteries and bewilderments of existence. He took the beautiful woman in his arms and kissed her.

"This is real and right, if anything is," said he. "If there are ghosts about, you and I, at any rate, are flesh and blood, and where we belong. As to the irrigation scrape, there must be some way out of it: if not, no matter! You and I love each other, and the world begins from this moment!"

"My father must know to-morrow," said Miriam.

"No doubt we shall all know more to- morrow than we do to-day," returned her lover, not knowing how abundantly his prophecy would be fulfilled: he was over- flowing with the fearless and enormous joy of a young man who has attained at one bound the summit of his desire. "There! they are calling for me. Good-by, my darling. Be yourself, and think of nothing but me."

A short ride brought the little cavalcade to the borders of the desert. Here, by common consent, a halt was made, to draw breath, as it were, before taking the final plunge into the fiery furnace.

"Before we go farther," said General Trednoke, approaching Freeman, as he was tightening his girths, "I must tell you what is the object of this expedition."

"It is not necessary, general," replied the young man, straightening himself and looking the other in the face; "for from this point our paths lie apart."

"Why so?" demanded the general, in surprise.

"What's that?" exclaimed Meschines, coming up, and adjusting his spectacles.

"I'm not at liberty, at present, to explain," Freeman answered. "All I can say is that I don't feel justified in assisting you in your affair, and I am not able to confide my own to you. I wish you to put the least uncharitable construction you can on my conduct. To-morrow, if we all live, I may say more; now, the most I can tell you is that I am not entirely a free agent. Meantime—Hasta luego."

Against this unexpected resolve the general cordially protested and the professor scoffed and contended; but Freeman stayed firm. He had with him provisions enough to last him three days, and a supply of water; and in a small case he carried a compact assortment of instruments for scientific observation. "Take your departure in whatever direction you like," said he, "and I will take mine at an angle of not less than fifteen degrees from it. If I am not back in three days, you may conclude something has happened."

It was certainly very hot. Freeman had been accustomed to torrid suns in the Isthmus; but this was a sun indefinitely multiplied by reflections from the dusty surface underfoot. Nor was it the fine, ethereal fire of the Sahara: the atmosphere was dead and heavy; for the rider was already far below the level of the Pacific, whose cool blue waves rolled and rippled many leagues to the westward, as, aeons ago, they had rolled and rippled here. There was not a breath of air. Freeman could hear his heart beat, and the veins in his temples and wrists throbbed. The sweat rose on the surface of his body, but without cooling it. The pony which he bestrode, a bony and sinewy beast of the toughest description, trod onwards doggedly, but with little animation. Freeman had no desire to push him. Were the little animal to overdo itself, nothing in the future could be more certain than that his master would never see the Trednoke ranch again. It seemed unusually hot, even for that region.

There was little in the way of outward incident to relieve the monotony of the journey. Now and then a short, thick rattlesnake, with horns on its ugly head, wriggled out of his path. Now and then his horse's hoof almost trod upon a hideous, flat lizard, also horned. Here and there the uncouth projections of a cactus pushed upwards out of the dust; some of these the mustang nibbled at, for the sake of their juice. Freeman wondered where the juice came from. The floor of the desert seemed for the most part level, though there was a gradual dip towards the east and northeast, and occasionally mounds and ridges of wind-swept dust, sometimes upwards of fifty feet in height, broke the uniformity. The soil was largely composed of powdered feldspar; but there were also tracts of gravel shingle, of yellow loam, and of alkaline dust. In some places there appeared a salt efflorescence, sprouting up in a sort of ghastly vegetation, as if death itself had acquired a sinister life. Elsewhere, the ground quaked and yielded underfoot, and it became necessary to make detours to avoid these arid bogs. Once or twice, too, Freeman turned aside lest he should trample upon some dry bones that protruded in his path,—bones that were their own monument, and told their own story of struggle, agony, exhaustion, and despair.

None of these things had any depressing effect on Freeman's spirit. His heart was singing with joy. To a mind logically disposed, there was nothing but trouble in sight, whether he succeeded or failed in his present mission. In the former case, he would find himself in a hostile position as regarded the man he most desired to conciliate; in the latter, he would remain the mere rolling stone that he was before, and love itself would forbid him to ask the woman he loved to share his uncertain existence. But Freeman was not logical: he was happy, and he could not help it. He had kissed Miriam, and she loved him.

His course lay a few degrees north of east. Far across the plain, dancing and turning somersaults in the fantastic atmosphere, were the summits of a range of abrupt hills, the borders of a valley or ravine which he wished to explore. Gradually, as he rode, his shadow lengthened before him. It was his only companion; and yet he felt no sense of loneliness. Miriam was in his heart, and kept it fresh and bold. Even hunger and thirst he scarcely felt. Who can estimate the therapeutic and hygienic effects of love?

The mustang could not share his rider's source of content, but he may have been conscious, through animal instincts whereof we know nothing, of an uplifting and encouraging spirit. At all events, he kept up his steady lope without faltering or apparent effort, and seemed to require nothing more than the occasional wetting which Freeman administered to his nose. There would probably be some vegetation, and perhaps water, on the hills; and that prospect may likewise have helped him along.

Nevertheless, man and beast may well have welcomed the hour when the craggy acclivities of that lonely range became so near that they seemed to loom above their heads. Freeman directed his steps towards the southern extremity, where a huge, pallid mass, of almost regular pyramidal form, reared itself aloft like a monument. He skirted the base of the pyramid, and there opened on his view a narrow, winding valley, scarcely half a mile in apparent breadth, and of a very wild and savage aspect. Its general direction was nearly north and south, and it declined downwards, as if seeking the interior of the earth. In fact, it looked not unlike those imaginative pictures of the road to the infernal regions described by the ancient poets. One could picture Pluto in his chariot, with Proserpine beside him, thundering downwards behind his black horses, on the way to those sombre and magnificent regions which are hollowed out beneath the surface of the planet.

Freeman, however, presently saw a sight which, if less spectacularly impressive, was far more agreeable to his eyes. On a shelf or cup of the declivity was a little clump of vegetation, and in the midst of it welled up a thin stream of water. The mustang scrambled eagerly towards it, and, before Freeman had had time to throw himself out of the saddle, he had plunged his muzzle into the rivulet. He sucked it down with such satisfaction that it was evident the water was not salt. Freeman laid himself prone upon the brink, and followed his steed's example. The draught was cool and pure.

"I didn't know how much I wanted it!" said he to himself. "It must come from a good way down. If I could only bring the parent stream to the surface, my mission would be on a fair road to success."

An examination of the spring revealed the fact that it could not have been long in existence. Indeed, there were no traces whatever of long continuance. The aperture in the rock through which it trickled bore the appearance of having been recently opened; fragments were lying near it that seemed to have been just broken off. The bed of the little stream was entirely free from moss or weeds; and after proceeding a short distance it dwindled and disappeared, either sucked up in vapor by the torrid air, or absorbed into the dusty soil. Manifestly, it was a recent creation.

"And, to be sure, why not?" ejaculated Freeman. "There was an earthquake last night, which swallowed up the spring in the Trednokes' garden: probably that same earthquake brought this stream to light. It vanished there, to reappear here. Well, the loss is not important to them, but the gain is very important to me. It is as if Miriam had come with a cup of water to refresh her lover in the desert. God bless her! She has refreshed me indeed, soul and body!"

He removed the saddle from the mustang, and turned him loose to make the best of such scanty herbage as he could find. Then he unpacked his own provisions, and made a comfortable meal; after which he rolled a cigarette and reclined on the spot most available, to rest and recuperate. The valley, or gorge, lay before him in the afternoon light. It was a strange and savage spectacle. Had it been torn asunder by some stupendous explosion, it could not have presented a rougher or more chaotic aspect. To look at it was like beholding the secret places of the earth. The rocky walls were of different colors, yellow, blue, and red, in many shades and gradations. They towered ruggedly upwards, sharply shadowed and brightly lighted, mounting in regular pinnacles, parting in black crevices; here and there vast masses hung poised on bases seemingly insufficient, ready to topple over on the unwary passer beneath. A short distance to the northward the ravine had a turn, and a projecting promontory hid its further extreme from sight. Freeman made up his mind to follow it up on foot, after the descending sun should have thrown a shadow over it. The indications, in his judgment, were not without promise that a system of judiciously-applied blastings might open up a source of water that would transform this dreadful barrenness into something quite different.

The shade of the great pyramid fell upon him as he lay, but the tumultuous wall opposite was brilliantly illuminated: the sky, over it, was of a peculiar brassy hue, but entirely cloudless. The radiations from the baked surface, ascending vertically, made the rocky bastion seem to quiver, as if it were a reflection cast on undulating water. The wreaths of tobacco-smoke that emanated from Freeman's mouth also ascended, until they touched the slant of sunlight overhead. As the young man's eyes followed these, something happened that caused him to utter an exclamation and raise himself on one arm.

All at once, in the vacant air diagonally above him, a sort of shadowy shimmer seemed to concentrate itself, which was rapidly resolved into color and form. It was much as if some unseen artist had swept a mass of mingled hues on a canvas and then had worked them with magical speed into a picture. There appeared a breadth of rolling country, covered with verdure, and in the midst of it the white walls and long, shadowed veranda of an adobe house. Freeman saw the vines clambering over the eaves and roof, the vases of earthenware suspended between the pillars and overflowing with flowers, the long windows, the steps descending into the garden. Now a figure clad in white emerged from the door and advanced slowly to the end of the veranda. He recognized the gait and bearing: he could almost fancy he discerned the beloved features. She stood there for a moment, gazing, as it seemed, directly at him. She raised her hands, and pressed them to her lips, then threw them outwards, with a gesture eloquent of innocent and tender passion. Freeman's heart leaped: involuntarily he stretched out his arms, and murmured, "Miriam!" The next moment, a tall, dark figure, with white hair, wrapped in a blanket, came stalking behind her, and made a beckoning movement. Miriam did not turn, but her bearing changed; her hands fell to her sides; she seemed bewildered. Freeman sprang angrily to his feet: the picture became blurred; it flowed into streaks of vague color; it was gone. There were only the brassy sky, and the painted crags quivering in the heat.

"That was not a mirage: it was a miracle," muttered the young man to himself. "Forty miles at least, and it seemed scarcely three hundred yards! What does it mean?"

The sun sank behind the hills, and a transparent shadow filled the gorge. Freeman, uneasy in mind, and unable to remain inactive, filled his canteen at the spring, and descended to the rugged trail at the bottom. Clambering over boulders, leaping across narrow chasms, letting himself down from ledges, his preoccupation soon left him, and physical exertion took the precedence. Half an hour's work brought him to the out- jutting promontory which had concealed the further reaches of the valley. These now lay before him, merging imperceptibly into indistinctness.

"This atmosphere is unbearable," said Freeman. "I must get a little higher up." He turned to the right, and saw a natural archway, of no great height, formed in the rock. The arch itself was white; the super- incumbent stone was of a dull red hue. On the left flank of the arch were a series of inscribed characters, which might have been cut by a human hand, or might have been a mere natural freak. They looked like some rude system of hieroglyphics, and bore no meaning to Freeman's mind.

A sort of crypt or deep recess was hollowed out beneath the arch, the full extent of which Freeman was unable to discern. The floor of it descended in ridges, like a rough staircase. He stood for a few moments peering into the gloom, tempted by curiosity to advance, but restrained partly by the gathering darkness, and partly by the oppressiveness of the atmosphere, which produced a sensation of giddiness. Something white gleamed on the threshold of the crypt. He picked it up. It was a human skull; but even as he lifted it it came apart in his hands and crumbled into fragments. Freeman's nerves were strong, but he shuddered slightly. The loneliness, the silence, the mystery, and the strange light-headedness that was coming over him combined to make him hesitate. "I'll

Julian Hawthorne

come back to-morrow morning early," he said to himself.

As if in answer, a deep, appalling roar broke forth apparently under his feet, and went rolling and reverberating up and down the canon. It died away, but was immediately followed by another yet more loud, and the ground shook and swayed beneath his feet. A gigantic boulder, poised high up on the other side of the canon, was unseated, and fell with a terrific crash. A hot wind swept sighing through the valley, and the air rapidly became dark. Again came the sigh, rising to a shriek, with roarings and thunderings that seemed to proceed both from the heavens and from the earth.

A dazzling flash of lightning split the air, bathing it for an instant in the brightness of day: in that instant Freeman saw the bolt strike the great white pyramid and splinter its crest into fragments, while the whole surface of the gorge heaved and undulated like a stormy sea. He had been staggering as best he might to a higher part of the ravine; but now he felt a stunning blow on his head: he fell, and knew no more.

CHAPTER VII

Two horsemen, one of whom led a third horse, carrying a pack-saddle, had reached the borders of the desert just as the earthquake began. When the first shock came, they were riding past a grove of live- oaks: they immediately dismounted, made fast their horses, and lay down beside some bushes that skirted the grove. Neither the earthquake nor the storm was so severe as was the case farther eastward. In an hour all was over, and they remounted and continued their journey, guiding their course by the stars.

"It was thus that we rode before, Kamaiakan," remarked the younger of the two travellers. "Yonder bright star stood as it does now, and the hour of the night was the same. But this shaking of the earth makes me fear for the safety of that youth. The sands of the desert may have swept over him; or he may have perished in the hills."

"The purposes of the gods cannot be altered, Semitzin," replied the old Indian, who perhaps would not have much regretted such a calamity as she suggested: it would be a simple solution of difficulties which might otherwise prove embarrassing. "It is my prayer, at all events, that the entrance to the treasure may not be closed."

"I care nothing for the treasure, unless I may share it with him," she returned. "Since we spoke together beside the fountain, I have seen him. He looked upon me doubtfully, being, perhaps, perplexed because of these features of the child Miriam, which I am compelled to wear."

"Truly, princess, what is he, that you should think of him?" muttered Kamaiakan.

"He satisfies my heart," was the reply.

"And I am resolved never again to give up this mortal habitation to her you call its rightful owner. I will never again leave this world, which I enjoy, for the unknown darkness out of which you called me."

"Princess, the gods do not permit such dealings. They may, indeed, suffer you to live again; but you must return as an infant, in flesh and bones of your own."

"The gods have permitted me to return as I have returned; and you well know, Kamaiakan, that, except you use your art to banish me and restore Miriam, there is nothing else that can work a change."

"Murder is not lawful, Semitzin; and to do as you desire would be an act not different from murder."

"On my head be it, then!" exclaimed the princess. "Would it be less a murder to send me back to nothingness than to let her remain there? Mine is the stronger spirit, and has therefore the better right to live. I ask of you only to do nothing. None need ever know that Miriam has vanished and that Semitzin lives in her place. I wear her body and her features, and I am content to wear her name also, if it must be so."

Kamaiakan was silent. He may well be pardoned for feeling troubled in the presence of a situation which had perhaps never before confronted a human being. Two women, both tenants of the same body, both in love with the same man, and therefore rivals of each other, and each claiming a right to existence: it was a difficult problem. The old Indian heartily wished that a separate tenement might be provided for each of these two souls, that they might fight out their quarrel in the ordinary way. But his magic arts did not extend to the creation of flesh and blood. At the same time, he could not but feel to blame for having brought this strenuous spirit of Semitzin once more into the world, and he was fain to admit that her claim was not without justification. His motives had been excellent, but he had not foreseen the consequences in which the act was to land him. Yet he more shrank from wronging Miriam than from disappointing Semitzin.

But the latter was not to be put off by silence.

"There has been a change since you and I last spoke together," she said. "I am aware of it, though I know not how; but, in some manner, the things which Miriam has done are perceptible to me. When I was here before, she did but lean towards this youth; now she has given herself to him. She means to be united to him; and, if I again should vanish, I should never again find my way back. But it shall not be so; and there is a way, Kamaiakan, by which I can surely prevent it, even though you refuse to aid me."

"Indeed, princess, I think you mistake regarding the love of Miriam for this young man; they have seen little of each other; and it may be, as you yourself said, that he has perished in the wilderness."

"I believe he lives," she answered: "I should know it, were it

Julian Hawthorne

otherwise. But if I cannot have him, neither shall she. I have told you already that, unless you swear to me not to put forth your power upon me to dismiss me, I will not lead you to the treasure. But that is not enough; for men deceive, and you are a man. But if at any time hereafter I feel within me those pangs that tell me you are about to separate me from this world, at that moment, Kamaiakan, I will drive this knife through the heart of Miriam! If I cannot keep her body, at least it shall be but a corpse when I leave it. You know Semitzin; and you know that she will keep her word!"

She reined in her horse, as she spoke, and sat gazing upon her companion with flashing eyes. The Indian, after a pause, made a gesture of gloomy resignation. "It shall be as you say, then, Semitzin; and upon your head be it! Henceforth, Miriam is no more. But do you beware of the vengeance of the gods, whose laws you have defied."

"Let the gods deal with me as they will," replied the Aztecan. "A day of happiness with the man I love is worth an age of punishment."

Kamaiakan made no answer, and the two rode forward in silence.

It was midnight, and a bright star, nearly in the zenith, seemed to hang precisely above the summit of the great white pyramid at the mouth of the gorge.

"It was here that we stopped," observed Semitzin. "We tied our horses among the shrubbery round yonder point. Thence we must go on foot. Follow me."

She struck her heels against her horse's sides, and went forward. The long ride seemed to have wearied her not a whit. The lean and wiry Indian had already betrayed symptoms of fatigue; but the young princess appeared as fresh as when she started. Not once had she even taken a draught from her canteen; and yet she was closely clad, from head to foot, in the doublet and leggings of the Golden Fleece. One might have thought it had some magic virtue to preserve its wearer's vitality; and possibly, as is sometimes seen in trance, the energy and concentration of the spirit reacted upon the body.

She turned the corner of the pyramid, but had not ridden far when an object lying in her path caused her to halt and spring from the saddle. Kamaiakan also dismounted and came forward.

The dead body of a mustang lay on the ground, crushed beneath the weight of a fragment of rock, which had evidently fallen upon it from a height. He had apparently been dead for some hours. He was without either saddle or bridle.

"Do you know him?" demanded Semitzin.

"It is Diego," replied Kamaiakan. "I know him by the white star on his muzzle. He was ridden by the Senor Freeman. They must have come here before the earthquake. And there lie the saddle and the bridle. But where is Senor Freeman?"

"He can be nowhere else than in this valley," said Semitzin, confidently. "I knew that I should find him here. Through all the centuries, and across all spaces, we were destined to meet. His horse was killed, but he has escaped. I shall save him. Could Miriam have done this? Is he not mine by right?"

"It is at least certain, princess," responded the old man rather dryly, "that had it not been for Miriam you would never have met the Senor Freeman at all."

"I thank her for so much; and some time, perhaps, I will reward her by permitting her to have a glimpse of him for an hour,—or, at least, a minute. But not now, Kamaiakan,—not till I am well assured that no thought but of me can ever find its way into his heart. Come, let us go forward. We will find the treasure, and I will give it to my lord and lover."

"Shall we bring the pack-horse with us?" asked the Indian.

"Yes, if he can find his way among these rocks. The earthquake has made changes here. See how the water pours from this spring! It has already made a stream down the valley. It shall guide us whither we are going."

Leaving their own horses, they advanced with the mule. But the trail, rough enough at best, was now well-nigh impassable. Masses of rock had fallen from above; large fissures and crevasses had been formed in the floor of the gorge, from some of which steaming vapors escaped, while others gave forth streams of water. The darkness added to the difficulties of the way, for, although the sky was now clear, the gloom was deceptive, and things distant seemed near. Occasionally a heavy, irregular sound would break the stillness, as some projection of a cliff became loosened and tumbled down the steep declivity.

Semitzin, however, held on her way fearlessly and without hesitation, and the Indian, with the pack-horse, followed as best he might, now and then losing sight for a moment of the slight, grayish figure in front of him. At length she disappeared behind the jutting profile of a great promontory which formed a main angle of the gorge. When he came up with her, she was kneeling beside the prostrate form of a man, supporting his head upon her knee.

Kamaiakan approached, and looked at the face of the man,

which was pale; the eyes were closed. A streak of blood, from a wound on the head, descended over the right side of the forehead.

"Is he dead?" the Indian asked.

"He is not dead," replied Semitzin. "A flying stone has struck him; but his heart beats: he will be well again." She poured some water from her canteen over his face, and bent her ear over his lips. "He breathes," she said. Slipping one arm beneath his neck, she loosened the shirt at his throat and then stooped and kissed him. "Be alive for me, love," she murmured. "My life is yours."

This exhortation seemed to have some effect. The man stirred slightly, and emitted a sigh. Presently he muttered, "I can—lick him—yet!"

"He will live, princess," remarked Kamaiakan. "But where is the treasure?"

"My treasure is here!" was her reply; and again she bent to kiss the half-conscious man, who knew not of his good fortune. After an interval she added, "It is in the hollow beneath that archway. Go down three paces: on the wall at the left you will feel a ring. Pull it outwards, and the stone will give way. Behind it lies the chest in which the jewels are. But remember your promise!"

Kamaiakan peered into the hollow, shook his head as one who loves not his errand, and stepped in. The black shadow swallowed him up. Semitzin paid no further attention to him, but was absorbed in ministering to her patient, whose strength was every moment being augmented, though he was not yet aware of his position. But all at once a choking sound came from within the cave, and in a few moments

Julian Hawthorne

Kamaiakan staggered up out of the shadow, and sank down across the threshold of the arch.

"Semitzin," he gasped, in a faint voice, "the curse of the gods is upon the spot! The air within is poisonous. It withers the limbs and stops the breath. No one may touch the treasure and live. Let us go!"

"The gods do not love those who fear," replied the princess, contemptuously. "But the treasure is mine, and it may well be that no other hand may touch it. Fold that blanket, and lay it beneath his head. I will bring the jewels."

"Do not attempt it: it will be death!" exclaimed the old man.

"Shall a princess come to her lover empty-handed? Do you watch beside him while I go. Ah, if your Miriam were here, I would not fear to have him choose between us!"

With these words, Semitzin stepped across the threshold of the crypt, and vanished in its depths. The Indian, still dizzy and faint, knelt on the rock without, bowed down by sinister forebodings.

Several minutes passed. "She has perished!" muttered Kamaiakan.

Freeman raised himself on one elbow, and gazed giddily about him. "What the deuce has happened?" he demanded, in a sluggish voice. "Is that you, professor?"

Suddenly, a rending and rushing sound burst from the cave. Following it, Semitzin appeared at the entrance, dragging a heavy metal box, which she grasped by a handle at one end. Immediately in her steps broke forth a great volume of water, boiling up as if from a caldron. It filled the cave, and poured like a cataract into the gorge. The foundations of the great deep seemed to be let loose.

Semitzin lifted from her face the woollen mask, or visor, which she had closed on entering the cave. She was panting from exertion, but neither her physical nor her mental faculties were abated. She spoke sharply and imperiously:

"Bring up the mule, and help me fasten the chest upon him. We must reach higher ground before the waters overtake us. And now—" She turned to Freeman, who by this time was sitting up and regarding her with stupefaction.

"Miriam!" was all he could utter.

She shook her head, and smiled. "I am she who loves you, and whom you will love. I give you life, and fortune, and myself. But come: can you mount and ride?"

"I can't make this out," he said, struggling, with her assistance, to his feet. "I have read fairy-tales, but this . . . Kamaiakan, too!"

Semitzin, meanwhile, brought him to the mule, and half mechanically he scrambled into the saddle, the chest being made fast to the crupper. Semitzin seized the bridle, and started up the gorge, Kamaiakan bringing up the rear. The lower levels were already filling with water, which came pouring out through the archway in a full flood, seemingly inexhaustible.

"I see how it is," mumbled Freeman, half to himself. "The earthquake—I remember! I got hit somehow. They came from the ranch to hunt me up. But where are the general and Professor Meschines? How long ago was it? And how came Miriam . . . Could the mirage have had anything to do with it?—Here, let me walk," he called out to her, "and you get up and ride."

She turned her head, smiling again, but hurried on without speaking. The roar of the torrent followed them. Once or twice the mule came near losing his footing. Freeman, whose head was swimming, and his brains buzzing like a hive of bees, had all he could do to maintain his equilibrium in the saddle. He was excruciatingly thirsty, and the gurgling of waters round about made him wish he might dismount and plunge into them. But he lacked power to form a decided purpose, and permitted the more energetic will to control him. It might have been minutes, or it might have been hours, for all he knew: at last they halted, near the base of the white pyramid.

"Here we are safe," said Semitzin, coming to his side. "Lean on me, my love, and I will lift you down."

"Oh, I'm not quite so bad as that, you know," said Freeman, with a feeble laugh; and, to prove it, he blundered off the saddle, and came down on the ground with a thwack. He picked himself up, however, and recollecting that he had a flask with brandy in it, he felt for it, found it intact, and, with an inarticulate murmur of apology, raised it to his lips. It was like the veritable elixir of life: never in his life before had Freeman quaffed so deep a draught of the fiery spirit. It was just what he wanted.

But he felt oddly embarrassed. He did not know what to make of Miriam. It was not her strange costume merely, but she seemed to have put on—or put off—something with it that made a difference in her. She was assertive, imperious; as loving, certainly, as lover could wish, but not in the manner of the Miriam he knew. He might have liked the new Miriam better, had he not previously fallen in love with the former one. He could not make advances to her: he had no opportunity to do so: she was making advances to him!

"My love," she said, standing before him, "I have come back to the world for your sake. Before Semitzin first saw you, her heart was yours. And I come to you, not poor, but with the riches and power of the princes of Tenochtitlan. You shall see them: they are yours!—Kamaiakan, take down the chest."

"What's that about Semitzin?" inquired Freeman. "I'm not aware that I knew any such person."

"Kamaiakan!" repeated the other, raising her voice, and not hearing Freeman's last words. Kamaiakan was nowhere to be seen. Both Freeman and she had supposed that he was following on behind the mule; but he had either dropped behind, or had withdrawn somewhere. "O Kamaiakan!" shouted Freeman, as loud as he could.

A distant hail, from the direction of the desert, seemed to reply.

"That can't be he," said Freeman. "It was at least a quarter of a mile off, and the wrong direction, too. He's in the gorge, if he's anywhere."

"Hark!" said Semitzin.

They listened, and detected a low murmur, this time from the gorge.

"He's fallen down and hurt himself," said Freeman. "Let's go after him."

In a few moments they stumbled upon the old Indian,

reclining with his shoulders against a rock, and gasping heavily.

"My princess," he whispered, as she bent over him, "I am dying. The poisonous air in the cave was fatal to me, though the spell that is upon the Golden Fleece protected you. I have done what the gods commanded. I am absolved of my vow. The treasure is safe."

"Nonsense! you're all right!" exclaimed Freeman. "Here, take a pull at this flask. It did me all the good in the world!"

But the old man put it aside, with a feeble gesture of the hand. "My time is come,—" said he.—"Semitzin, I have been faithful."

"Semitzin, again!" muttered Freeman. "What does it mean?"

"But what is this?" cried the girl, suddenly starting to her feet. "I feel the sleep coming on me again! I feel Miriam returning! Kamaiakan, have you betrayed me at the last?"

"No, no, princess, I have done nothing," said he, in a voice scarcely audible. "But, with death, the strength of my will goes from me, and I can no longer keep you in this world. The spirit of Miriam claims her rightful body, and you must struggle against her alone. The gods will not be defied: it is the law!"

His voice sank away into nothing, and his beard drooped upon his breast.

"He's dying, sure enough, poor old chap," said Freeman. "But what is all this about? I never heard anything like this language you two talk together."

Semitzin turned towards him, and her eyes were blazing.

"She shall not have you!" she cried. "I have won you—I have saved you—you are mine! What is Miriam? Can she be to you what I could be?—You shall never have him!" she continued, seeming to address some presence invisible to all eyes but hers. "If I must go, you shall go with me!" She fumbled in her belt, caught the handle of a knife there, and drew it. She lifted it against her heart; but even then there was an uncertainty in her movement, as if her mind were divided against itself, or had failed fully to retain the thread of its purpose. But Freeman, who had passed rapidly from one degree of bewilderment to another, was actually relieved to see, at last, something that he could understand. Miriam— for some reason best known to herself—was about to do herself a mischief. He leaped forward, caught her in his arms, and snatched the knife from her grasp.

For a few moments she struggled like a young tiger. And it was marvellous and appalling to hear two voices come from her, in alternation, or confusedly mingled. One said, "Let me kill her! I will not go! Keep back, you pale-faced girl!" and then a lower, troubled voice, "Do not let her come! Her face is terrible! What are those strange creatures with her? Harvey, where are you?"

At last, with a fierce cry, that died away in a shuddering sigh, the form of flesh and blood, so mysteriously possessed, ceased to struggle, and sank back in Freeman's arms. His own strength was well-nigh at an end. He laid her on the ground, and, sitting beside her, drew her head on his knee. He had been in the land of spirits, contending with unknown powers, and he was faint in mind and body.

Yet he was conscious of the approaching tread of horses' feet, and recollected the hail that had come from the desert.

Soon loomed up the shadowy figures of mounted men, and they came so near that he was constrained to call out, "Mind where you're going! You'll be over us!"

"Who are you?" said a voice, which sounded like that of General Trednoke, as they reined up.

"There's Kamaiakan, who's dead; and Miriam Trednoke, who has been out of her mind, but she's got over it now, I guess; and I,—Harvey Freeman."

"My daughter!" exclaimed General Trednoke.

"My boy!" cried Professor Meschines. "Well, thank God we've found you, and that some of you are alive, at any rate!"

CHAPTER VIII

As it was still some hours before dawn, and Freeman was too weak to travel, it was decided to encamp beside the pyramid till the following evening, and then make the trip across the desert in the comparative coolness of starlight. Meanwhile, there was something to be done, and much to be explained.

The spirit of Kamaiakan had passed away, apparently at the same moment that the peculiar case of "possession" under which Miriam had suffered came to an end. They determined to bury him at the foot of the great pyramid, which would form a fitting monument of his antique character and virtues.

Miriam, after her struggle, had lapsed into a state of partial lethargy, from which she was aroused gradually. It was then found that she could give no account what ever of how or why she came there. The last thing she distinctly remembered was standing on the veranda at the ranch and looking towards the east. She was under the impression that Kamaiakan had approached and spoken with her, but of that she was not certain. The next fact in her consciousness was that she was held in Freeman's arms, with a feeling that she had barely escaped from some great peril. She could recall nothing of the journey down the gorge, of the adventure at the bottom of it, or of the return. It was only by degrees that some partial light was thrown upon this matter. Freeman knew that he was at the entrance of the cave when the earthquake began, and he remembered receiving a blow on the head. Consequently it must have been at that spot that Miriam and the Indian found him. He had, too, a vague impression of seeing Miriam coming out of the cave, dragging the chest; and there, sure enough, was a metal box, strapped to the saddle of the pack-mule. But the mystery remained very dense. And although the reader is in a position to analyze events more closely than the actors themselves could do, it may be doubted whether the essential mystery is much clearer to him than it was to them.

"We know that the ancient Aztecan priests were adepts in magic," observed the professor, "and it's natural that some of their learning should have descended to their posterity. We have been clever in giving names to such phenomena, but we know perhaps even less about their esoteric meaning than the Aztecans did. I should judge that Miriam would be what is called a good 'subject.' Kamaiakan discovered that fact; and as for what followed, we can only infer it from the results. I was always an admirer of Kamaiakan; but I must say I am the better resigned to his departure, from the reflection that Miriam will henceforth be undisturbed in the possession of her own individuality."

"As near as I could make out, she called herself Semitzin," put in Freeman.

"Semitzin?" repeated the general. "Why, if I'm not mistaken, there are accounts of an Aztecan princess of that name, an ancestress of my wife's family, in some old documents that I have in a box, at home."

"That would only add the marvel of heredity to the other marvels," said Meschines. "Suppose we leave the things we can't understand, and come to those we can?"

"I have something to say, General Trednoke," said Freeman.

"I think I have already guessed what it may be, Mr. Freeman," returned the general, gravely. "Old people have eyes, and hearts too, as well as young ones."

"Come, Trednoke," interposed the professor, with a chuckle, "your eyes might not have seen so much, if I hadn't held the lantern."

"I love your daughter, and I told her so yesterday morning," went on Freeman, after a pause. "I meant to tell you on my return. I know I don't appear desirable as a son-in-law. But I came here on a commission—"

"Meschines and I have talked it all over," the general said. "When an old West-Pointer and a professor of physics get together, they are sometimes able to put two and two together. And, to tell the truth, I received a letter from a member of your syndicate, who is also an acquaintance of mine, which explained your position. Under the circumstances, I consider your course to have been honorable. You and I were both in search of the same thing, and now, as it appears, nature has sent an earthquake to do our affair for us. No operations of ours could have achieved such a result as last night's disturbance did; and if that do not prove effective, nothing else will."

"If it turns out well, I was promised a share in the benefits," said Freeman, "and that would put me in a rather better condition, from a worldly point of view."

"After all," interrupted Meschines, "you found your way to the spot from which the waters broke forth, and may fairly be entitled to the credit of the discovery.—Eh, Trednoke? At any rate, we found nothing.—Yes, I think they'll have to admit you to partnership, Harvey: and Miriam too,—who, by the way, seems to be the only one who actually penetrated into this cave you speak of. Maybe the removal of the chest pulled the plug out of the bung-hole, as it were: the escape of confined air through such a vent would be apt to draw water along with it. By the way, let's have a look at this same chest: it looks solid enough to hold something valuable."

"I would like, in the first place, to hear what General Trednoke has to say about what I have told him," said Freeman, clearing his throat.

"Miriam," said the general, "do you wish to be married to this young man?"

The old soldier was sitting with her hand in his, and he turned to her as he spoke. She threw her arms round his neck, and pressed her face against his shoulder. "He is to me what you were to mamma," she said, so that only he could hear.

"Then be to him what she was to me," answered the general, kissing her. "Ah me, little girl! I am old, but perhaps this is the right way for me to grow young again. Well, if you are of the same mind six months hence—"

"Worse; it will be much worse, then," murmured the professor. "Better make it three."

The chest was made of some alloy of steel and nickel, impervious to rust, and very hard. It resisted all gentle methods of attack, and it was finally found necessary to force the lock with a charge of powder. Within was found another case, which was pried open with the point of the general's bowie-knife.

It was filled to the brim with precious stones, most of them removed from their settings. But such of the gold-work as remained showed the jewels to be of ancient Aztecan origin. There was value enough in the box to buy and stock a dozen ranches as big as the general's, and leave heirlooms enough to decorate a family larger than that of the most fruitful of the ancient patriarchs.

"I call that quite a respectable dowry," remarked Meschines. "Upon my soul, Miriam, if I had known what you had up your sleeve, I should have thought twice before allowing a 'civil engineer'—do you remember?—to run off with you so easily."

At dawn, they prepared the body of old Kamaiakan for its interment. In doing this, the professor noted the peculiar appearance of the corpse.

"The flesh is absolutely withered," said he, "especially those parts which were uncovered. It must have been subjected to the action of some destructive vapor or gas, fatal not only to breathe, but to come in contact with. I have heard of poisonous emanations proceeding from the ground in these regions, but I never saw an instance of their effects before. That skull that you say you found, Harvey, was probably that of a victim of the same cause. But it is strange that Miriam, who must have remained some time in the very midst of it, should have escaped without a mark, or even any inconvenience."

"Kamaiakan ascribed it to the magic of the Golden Fleece," said Freeman.

"Well," rejoined the other, "he may have been right; but, for my part, the only magic that I can find in it lies in the fact that it is made of pure wool, which undoubtedly possesses

Julian Hawthorne

remarkable sanative properties; or maybe the fiery soul of Semitzin was powerful enough to repel all harmful influences. The poor old fellow himself, being clad in cotton, and with no soul but his own, was destroyed. Let us wrap him in his blanket, and bid him farewell—and with him, I hope, to all that is uncanny and abnormal in the lives of you young folks!"

The last rites having been paid to the dead, the party mounted their horses and rode out of the gorge on to the long levels of the desert.

"Who come yonder?" said Freeman.

"A couple of Mexicans, I think," said the general.

"One of them is a woman," said Meschines.

"They look very weary," remarked Freeman.

Miriam fixed her eyes on the approaching pair for a moment, and then said, "They are Senor de Mendoza and Grace Parsloe."

And so, indeed, they were; and thus, in this lonely spot, all the dramatis personae of this history found themselves united.

In answer to the obvious question, how Grace and De Mendoza happened to be there, it transpired that, left to their own devices, they had undertaken no less an enterprise than to discover the hidden treasure. Grace had communicated to the Mexican such bits of information as she had picked up and such surmises as she had formed, and he had been able to supplement her knowledge to an extent that seemed to justify them in attempting the adventure,—not to mention the fact that Don Miguel (such was the ardor of his sentiment for Grace) would, had she desired it, have gone with her into a fiery furnace or a den of lions. Grace, who was ambitious as well as romantic, and who longed for the power and independence that wealth would give, was all alight with the idea of capturing the hoard of Montezuma: her social position would be altered at a stroke, and the world would be at her feet. Whether she would then have rewarded Don Miguel for his devotion, is possibly open to doubt: the sudden acquisition of boundless wealth has been known to turn larger heads than hers. Fortunately, however, this temptation was withheld from her: so far from finding the treasure, she and Don Miguel very soon lost themselves in the desert, and had been wandering about ever since, dolely uncomfortable, and in no small danger of losing their lives. They were already at the end of their last resource when they happened to encounter the other party, as we have seen; and immeasurable was their joy at the unlooked-for deliverance. So there was another halt, to enable them to rest and recuperate; and it was not until the evening of that day that the journey was finally resumed.

Meanwhile, Grace had time to think over all that happened, and to arrive at certain conclusions. She was at bottom a good girl, though liable to be led away by her imagination, her vanity, and her temperament. Don Miguel's best qualities had revealed themselves to her in the desert: he had always thought of her before himself, had done all that in him lay to save her from fatigue and suffering, and had stuck to her faithfully when he might perhaps have increased his own chances of escape by abandoning her. Did not such a man deserve to be rewarded?—especially as he was a handsome fellow, of good family, and possessed of quite a respectable income. Moreover, Harvey Freeman was now beyond her reach: he was going to marry Miriam, and she had realized that her own brief infatuation for him had had no very deep root after all. Accordingly, she smiled encouragingly upon Don Miguel, and before they set out on their homeward ride she had vouchsafed him the bliss of knowing that he might call her his.

The general, as her guardian, did not withhold his approval; but when Grace drew him aside and besought him never to reveal to her intended the fact that she had once been a shop-girl, the old warrior smiled.

"You can depend upon me to keep your secret, if you wish it, my dear," said he; "but I warn you that such concealments between husband and wife are not wise. He loves you and would only love you the more for your frankness in confessing what you seem to consider a discreditable episode: though I for my part am free to tell you that you will be lucky if your future life affords you the opportunity of doing anything else so much to your credit. But the chances are that he will find it out sooner or later; and that may not be so agreeable, either to him or to you. Better tell him all now."

But Grace pictured to herself the aristocratic pride of an hidalgo shocked by the suggestion of the plebeianism of trade; and she would not consent to the revelation. But the general's prediction was fulfilled sooner than might have been expected.

For, after they were married, Don Miguel decided to visit the Atlantic coast on the wedding journey; and one of the first notable places they reached was, of course, New York. Don Miguel was delighted, and was never weary of strolling up Fifth Avenue and down Broadway, with his beautiful wife on his arm. He marvelled at the vast white pile of the Fifth Avenue Hotel; he frowned at the Worth Monument; he stared inexhaustibly into the shop-windows; he exclaimed with admiration at the stupendous piles of masonry which contained the goods of New York's merchant princes. It seemed to be his opinion that the possessors of so much palpable wealth must be the true aristocracy of the country.

And one afternoon it happened that as they were strolling along Broadway, between Twenty-third Street and Union Square, and were crossing one of the side-streets, a horse belonging to one of Lord and Taylor's delivery- wagons became frightened, and bolted round the corner. One of the hind wheels of the vehicle came in contact with Grace's shoulder, and knocked her down. The blow and the fall stunned her. Don Miguel's grief and indignation were expressed with tropical energy; and a by-stander said, "Better carry her into the store, mister; it's their wagon run her down, and they can't do less than look after her."

The counsel seemed reasonable, and Don Miguel, with the assistance of a policeman, lifted his wife and bore her into the stately shop. One of the floor-walkers met them at the door; he cast a glance at their burden, and exclaimed, "Why, it's Miss Parsloe!" And immediately a number of the employees gathered round, all regarding her with interest and sympathy, all anxious to help, and—which was what mystified Don Miguel—all calling her by name! How came they to know Grace Parsloe? Nay, they even glanced at Don Miguel, as if to ask what was HIS business with the beautiful unconscious one!

"This lady are my wife," he said, with dignity. "She not any more Miss Parsloe."

"Oh, Grace has got married!" exclaimed the young ladies, one to another; and then an elderly man, evidently in authority, came forward and said, "I suppose you are aware, sir, that Miss Parsloe was formerly one of our girls here; and a very clever and useful girl she was. I need not say how sorry we are for this accident: I have sent for the physician: but I cannot but be glad that the misfortune has at least given me the opportunity of telling you how highly your wife was valued and respected here."

At this juncture, Grace opened her eyes: she looked from one face to another, and knew that fate had brought the truth to light. But the physical shock tempered the severity of the mental one: besides, she could not help being pleased at the sight of so many well-remembered and friendly faces; and, finally, her husband did not look by any means so angry and scandalized as she had feared he would. Indeed, he appeared almost gratified. The truth probably was, he was flattered to see his wife the centre of so much interest and attention, and at the discovery that she had been in some way an honored appanage of so imposing an establishment. So, by the time Grace was well enough to be driven back to her hotel, the senor was prattling cheerfully and familiarly with all and sundry, and was promising to bring his wife back there the next day, to talk over old times with her former associates.

Such was Grace's punishment: it was not very severe; but then her fault had been a venial one; and the episode was of much moral benefit to her. She liked her husband all the better for having nothing more to conceal from him; her vanity was rebuked, and her false pride chastened; and when, in after-years, her pretty daughters and black-haired sons gathered about her knees, she was wont to warn them sagely against the un-American absurdity of fearing to work for their living, or being ashamed to have it known.

But the married life of Miriam and Harvey Freeman was characteristically American in its happiness. The representatives of the oldest and of the latest inhabitants of this continent, their union seemed to produce the flower of what was best in both. Their wedding is still remembered in that region, as being everything that a Southern Californian wedding should be; and the bride, as she stood at the altar, looked what she was,—one of those women who, more than anything else in this world, are fitted to bring back to earth the gentle splendors of the Garden of Eden. In her dark eyes, as she fixed them upon Freeman, there was a mystic light, telling of fathomless depths of tenderness and intelligence: it seemed to her husband that love had expanded and uplifted her; or perhaps that other spirit in her, which had battled with her own, had now become reconciled, and therefore yielded up whatever it had of good and noble to aggrandize the gentle victory of its conqueror. Somehow, somewhere, in Miriam's nature, Semitzin lived; and, as a symbol of the peace and atonement that were the issue of her strange interior story, her husband preserves with reverence and affection the mysterious garment called the Golden Fleece.

Choose from Thousands of 1stWorldLibrary Classics By

A. M. Barnard
Ada Leverson
Adolphus William Ward
Aesop
Agatha Christie
Alexander Aaronsohn
Alexander Kielland
Alexandre Dumas
Alfred Gatty
Alfred Ollivant
Alice Duer Miller
Alice Turner Curtis
Alice Dunbar
Allen Chapman
Alleyne Ireland
Ambrose Bierce
Amelia E. Barr
Amory H. Bradford
Andrew Lang
Andrew McFarland Davis
Andy Adams
Angela Brazil
Anna Alice Chapin
Anna Sewell
Annie Besant
Annie Hamilton Donnell
Annie Payson Call
Annie Roe Carr
Annonaymous
Anton Chekhov
Archibald Lee Fletcher
Arnold Bennett
Arthur C. Benson
Arthur Conan Doyle
Arthur M. Winfield
Arthur Ransome
Arthur Schnitzler
Arthur Train
Atticus
B.H. Baden-Powell
B. M. Bower
B. C. Chatterjee
Baroness Emmuska Orczy
Baroness Orczy
Basil King
Bayard Taylor
Ben Macomber
Bertha Muzzy Bower
Bjornstjerne Bjornson

Booth Tarkington
Boyd Cable
Bram Stoker
C. Collodi
C. E. Orr
C. M. Ingleby
Carolyn Wells
Catherine Parr Traill
Charles A. Eastman
Charles Amory Beach
Charles Dickens
Charles Dudley Warner
Charles Farrar Browne
Charles Ives
Charles Kingsley
Charles Klein
Charles Hanson Towne
Charles Lathrop Pack
Charles Romyn Dake
Charles Whibley
Charles Willing Beale
Charlotte M. Braeme
Charlotte M. Yonge
Charlotte Perkins Stetson
Clair W. Hayes
Clarence Day Jr.
Clarence E. Mulford
Clemence Housman
Confucius
Coningsby Dawson
Cornelis DeWitt Wilcox
Cyril Burleigh
D. H. Lawrence
Daniel Defoe
David Garnett
Dinah Craik
Don Carlos Janes
Donald Keyhoe
Dorothy Kilner
Dougan Clark
Douglas Fairbanks
E. Nesbit
E. P. Roe
E. Phillips Oppenheim
E. S. Brooks
Earl Barnes
Edgar Rice Burroughs
Edith Van Dyne
Edith Wharton

Edward Everett Hale
Edward J. O'Biren
Edward S. Ellis
Edwin L. Arnold
Eleanor Atkins
Eleanor Hallowell Abbott
Eliot Gregory
Elizabeth Gaskell
Elizabeth McCracken
Elizabeth Von Arnim
Ellem Key
Emerson Hough
Emilie F. Carlen
Emily Bronte
Emily Dickinson
Enid Bagnold
Enilor Macartney Lane
Erasmus W. Jones
Ernie Howard Pie
Ethel May Dell
Ethel Turner
Ethel Watts Mumford
Eugene Sue
Eugenie Foa
Eugene Wood
Eustace Hale Ball
Evelyn Everett-green
Everard Cotes
F. H. Cheley
F. J. Cross
F. Marion Crawford
Fannie E. Newberry
Federick Austin Ogg
Ferdinand Ossendowski
Fergus Hume
Florence A. Kilpatrick
Fremont B. Deering
Francis Bacon
Francis Darwin
Frances Hodgson Burnett
Frances Parkinson Keyes
Frank Gee Patchin
Frank Harris
Frank Jewett Mather
Frank L. Packard
Frank V. Webster
Frederic Stewart Isham
Frederick Trevor Hill
Frederick Winslow Taylor

Friedrich Kerst
Friedrich Nietzsche
Fyodor Dostoyevsky
G.A. Henty
G.K. Chesterton
Gabrielle E. Jackson
Garrett P. Serviss
Gaston Leroux
George A. Warren
George Ade
Geroge Bernard Shaw
George Cary Eggleston
George Durston
George Ebers
George Eliot
George Gissing
George MacDonald
George Meredith
George Orwell
George Sylvester Viereck
George Tucker
George W. Cable
George Wharton James
Gertrude Atherton
Gordon Casserly
Grace E. King
Grace Gallatin
Grace Greenwood
Grant Allen
Guillermo A. Sherwell
Gulielma Zollinger
Gustav Flaubert
H. A. Cody
H. B. Irving
H.C. Bailey
H. G. Wells
H. H. Munro
H. Irving Hancock
H. R. Naylor
H. Rider Haggard
H. W. C. Davis
Haldeman Julius
Hall Caine
Hamilton Wright Mabie
Hans Christian Andersen
Harold Avery
Harold McGrath
Harriet Beecher Stowe
Harry Castlemon
Harry Coghill
Harry Houidini

Hayden Carruth
Helent Hunt Jackson
Helen Nicolay
Hendrik Conscience
Hendy David Thoreau
Henri Barbusse
Henrik Ibsen
Henry Adams
Henry Ford
Henry Frost
Henry James
Henry Jones Ford
Henry Seton Merriman
Henry W Longfellow
Herbert A. Giles
Herbert Carter
Herbert N. Casson
Herman Hesse
Hildegard G. Frey
Homer
Honore De Balzac
Horace B. Day
Horace Walpole
Horatio Alger Jr.
Howard Pyle
Howard R. Garis
Hugh Lofting
Hugh Walpole
Humphry Ward
Ian Maclaren
Inez Haynes Gillmore
Irving Bacheller
Isabel Cecilia Williams
Isabel Hornibrook
Israel Abrahams
Ivan Turgenev
J.G.Austin
J. Henri Fabre
J. M. Barrie
J. M. Walsh
J. Macdonald Oxley
J. R. Miller
J. S. Fletcher
J. S. Knowles
J. Storer Clouston
J. W. Duffield
Jack London
Jacob Abbott
James Allen
James Andrews
James Baldwin

James Branch Cabell
James DeMille
James Joyce
James Lane Allen
James Lane Allen
James Oliver Curwood
James Oppenheim
James Otis
James R. Driscoll
Jane Abbott
Jane Austen
Jane L. Stewart
Janet Aldridge
Jens Peter Jacobsen
Jerome K. Jerome
Jessie Graham Flower
John Buchan
John Burroughs
John Cournos
John F. Kennedy
John Gay
John Glasworthy
John Habberton
John Joy Bell
John Kendrick Bangs
John Milton
John Philip Sousa
John Taintor Foote
Jonas Lauritz Idemil Lie
Jonathan Swift
Joseph A. Altsheler
Joseph Carey
Joseph Conrad
Joseph E. Badger Jr
Joseph Hergesheimer
Joseph Jacobs
Jules Vernes
Julian Hawthrone
Julie A Lippmann
Justin Huntly McCarthy
Kakuzo Okakura
Karle Wilson Baker
Kate Chopin
Kenneth Grahame
Kenneth McGaffey
Kate Langley Bosher
Kate Langley Bosher
Katherine Cecil Thurston
Katherine Stokes
L. A. Abbot
L. T. Meade

L. Frank Baum
Latta Griswold
Laura Dent Crane
Laura Lee Hope
Laurence Housman
Lawrence Beasley
Leo Tolstoy
Leonid Andreyev
Lewis Carroll
Lewis Sperry Chafer
Lilian Bell
Lloyd Osbourne
Louis Hughes
Louis Joseph Vance
Louis Tracy
Louisa May Alcott
Lucy Fitch Perkins
Lucy Maud Montgomery
Luther Benson
Lydia Miller Middleton
Lyndon Orr
M. Corvus
M. H. Adams
Margaret E. Sangster
Margret Howth
Margaret Vandercook
Margaret W. Hungerford
Margret Penrose
Maria Edgeworth
Maria Thompson Daviess
Mariano Azuela
Marion Polk Angellotti
Mark Overton
Mark Twain
Mary Austin
Mary Catherine Crowley
Mary Cole
Mary Hastings Bradley
Mary Roberts Rinehart
Mary Rowlandson
M. Wollstonecraft Shelley
Maud Lindsay
Max Beerbohm
Myra Kelly
Nathaniel Hawthrone
Nicolo Machiavelli
O. F. Walton
Oscar Wilde

Owen Johnson
P.G. Wodehouse
Paul and Mabel Thorne
Paul G. Tomlinson
Paul Severing
Percy Brebner
Percy Keese Fitzhugh
Peter B. Kyne
Plato
Quincy Allen
R. Derby Holmes
R. L. Stevenson
R. S. Ball
Rabindranath Tagore
Rahul Alvares
Ralph Bonehill
Ralph Henry Barbour
Ralph Victor
Ralph Waldo Emmerson
Rene Descartes
Ray Cummings
Rex Beach
Rex E. Beach
Richard Harding Davis
Richard Jefferies
Richard Le Gallienne
Robert Barr
Robert Frost
Robert Gordon Anderson
Robert L. Drake
Robert Lansing
Robert Lynd
Robert Michael Ballantyne
Robert W. Chambers
Rosa Nouchette Carey
Rudyard Kipling
Saint Augustine
Samuel B. Allison
Samuel Hopkins Adams
Sarah Bernhardt
Sarah C. Hallowell
Selma Lagerlof
Sherwood Anderson
Sigmund Freud
Standish O'Grady
Stanley Weyman
Stella Benson
Stella M. Francis

Stephen Crane
Stewart Edward White
Stijn Streuvels
Swami Abhedananda
Swami Parmananda
T. S. Ackland
T. S. Arthur
The Princess Der Ling
Thomas A. Janvier
Thomas A Kempis
Thomas Anderton
Thomas Bailey Aldrich
Thomas Bulfinch
Thomas De Quincey
Thomas Dixon
Thomas H. Huxley
Thomas Hardy
Thomas More
Thornton W. Burgess
U. S. Grant
Upton Sinclair
Valentine Williams
Various Authors
Vaughan Kester
Victor Appleton
Victor G. Durham
Victoria Cross
Virginia Woolf
Wadsworth Camp
Walter Camp
Walter Scott
Washington Irving
Wilbur Lawton
Wilkie Collins
Willa Cather
Willard F. Baker
William Dean Howells
William le Queux
W. Makepeace Thackeray
William W. Walter
William Shakespeare
Winston Churchill
Yei Theodora Ozaki
Yogi Ramacharaka
Young E. Allison
Zane Grey